BREAKTHROUGH

THE STORY OF CHATHAM'S NORTH BEACH

TIMOTHY J. WOOD

HYORA PUBLICATIONS

BREAKTHROUGH: The Story of Chatham's North Beach
Published by Hyora Publications, Inc.
60C Munson Meeting Way
Chatham, Massachusetts, 02633 USA
in association with
Murray the Cat Productions

ISBN 0-9718363-0-2

Originally published 1988
Revised and reprinted 1995, 2002
Photo/illustration credits, page 109

Additional copies of BREAKTHROUGH may be ordered by sending $12.95 plus $2.50 for shipping to BREAKTHROUGH, 60C Munson Meeting Way, Chatham, MA 02633.
For more information, check out our Web sites:
www.capecodchronicle.com
www.murraythecat.com

PRINTED IN CANADA

CONTENTS

INTRODUCTION TO NEW EDITION...5

LIFE'S A BEACH...8

NATURE'S DESIGN: THE BARRIER BEACH CYCLE...........................12

THE GREAT BEACH...23

BREAKTHROUGH..45

BREACH...59

THE PLAYERS...65

ALL ALONG THE REVETMENT..89

RETURN OF THE REVETMENT WARS..99

GLOSSARY..106

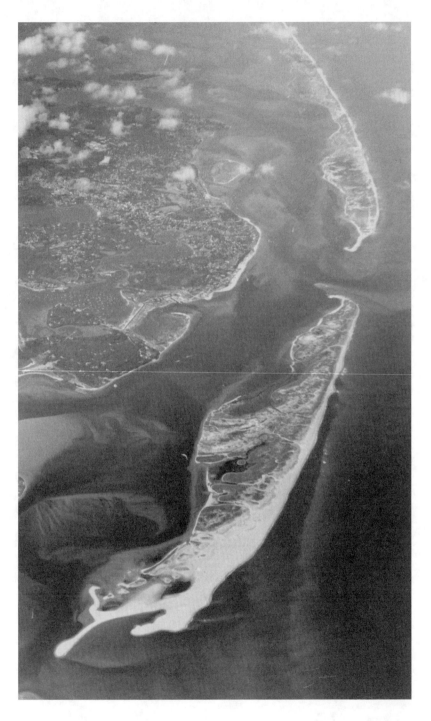

4**BREAKTHROUGH**

INTRODUCTION TO 2002 EDITION

A cozy seaside village like Chatham is the last place you'd expect to find the primeval war between man and nature raging like a full-blown northeaster. Yet that's just what has been happening here since 1987, when nature struck the first blow by gouging out a chunk of North Beach and allowing the hungry Atlantic access to the town's unprotected shoreline. After being grievously wounded, man fought back, and the opponents — old enemies, to be sure — now face each other in a stalemate, sure to be temporary.

This is the story of the conflict, told both as geologic history and social drama. One reason for its existence is so that future generations do not drop their guard and allow the enemy to sneak up on them, as it did in 1987. As sure as barrier beaches migrate, someone will come along in 50 or 75 years and claim he or she has a right to build a house between Andrew Harding's Lane and Holway Street, complete with fortifications against the inevitable, of an engineering design which we can only imagine today. Let that person and those like him or her be warned: beaches are transient and sand makes a poor foundation. It says so in the Bible, and many of us have seen it with our own eyes.

There are other reasons this story is being told. To set the record straight, for one. Even as houses were crashing to the beach, the history of the break and its results were being rewritten in court briefs and by certain segments of the media. At one point, erosion victims became a *cause celebre* and it was forgotten that they had chosen to buy homes where the land meets the sea and that no one ever guaranteed natural disaster wouldn't strike.

People have told me that earlier editions of *Breakthrough* were helpful in understanding not only the natural processes that go into the

Nauset Beach barrier beach system, but also the events that led up to the lawsuits and lost homes that were a direct result of the phenomenon. If I've succeeded, it's because the story is compelling on several levels: It has the scope of an epic and the drama of a tragedy, the fury of nature and the conceit of man, and it will not truly end for at least another 100 years, and then it will start all over again. The story at its most basic is both a denial and reaffirmation of the continuity of nature. It is also reassuring in that it shows that like man, the natural world, too, must go through cycles of birth and death. Usually, it moves at a geologic pace, spanning many human lifetimes, but sometimes conditions are right and the pace quickens. When that happens, those of us lucky to be alive get to experience nature in its true awesomeness.

* * *

In this sixth edition of *Breakthrough*, the text has been updated and errors in previous editions corrected. The last two chapters have been rewritten to bring the story up to late 2001. I've also added a glossary defining many of the technical and scientific terms used throughout the book which may be unfamiliar to the average reader, as well as a handy run-down of the major players in the drama.

Timothy J. Wood
Chatham, Massachusetts
November 2001

Before and After. Top, North Beach before the breakthrough. Below, the barrier beach in early 1987.

THE STORY OF CHATHAM'S NORTH BEACH

7

LIFE'S A BEACH

Snow had turned to intermittent, frigid rain by the early afternoon of January 2, 1987. Downtown Chatham was nearly deserted. I parked my car on Main Street and, leaning into gale force winds, made my way to the Mayflower Shop to pick up the Boston Globe. I plunked down my quarter and lingered, not exactly eager to venture back outside. Until Dan Ward, the shop's owner, called from behind a shelf, "Have you heard? The beach has broken through."

I hit the street running. This was news. Big news. The event nearly everyone in town had been anxiously expecting for years. When I arrived at the Lighthouse Beach overlook, camera in hand, a crowd had already gathered. A mile across the harbor, under dark, angry skies, violent breakers ignored the thin sand spit of North Beach and charged headlong toward the mainland. In the space of a few hours, one storm drastically altered the history of Chatham, reshaping the fate of scores of people for years to come.

* * *

Chatham has been described as a town virtually at sea. Its location, at the elbow of Cape Cod, 40 miles east of mainland Massachusetts, puts it farther out into the Atlantic Ocean than any other community in the nation. All 10½ square miles of mainland Chatham (Monomoy and North Beach contain another six or so square miles of upland) are essentially held prisoner by the sea. The town is circumscribed by 60 miles of shoreline, more than just about any other town in the Massachusetts, both a boon and a bane in the more than 300 years since Europeans first settled here. Aquatic resources, such as shell and fin fish, recreational activities and incomparable vistas are balanced by the often violent climate and the sometimes destructive whims of nature.

Into this small, ocean-ringed town are packed 6,500 year-round residents, more than half of whom are retired or elderly; according to the 2000 federal census, Chatham has the second highest median age in the state. The economy is heavily geared toward the summer tourist season, when the population balloons to more than 20,000, but it has diversified in recent years, thanks in large part to the influx of relatively affluent retirees, professionals and second homeowners. These days, you can actually find more than grocery, drug or liquor stores open during February and March, something that wasn't true 15 years ago. Chatham is also a major fishing center. It ranks fifth in fin fish landings among Massachusetts ports, and has remained relatively healthy despite government catch restrictions, thanks chiefly to the small-boat inshore fleet that specializes in a fresh, high quality product known throughout the region. Some $5 million worth of shellfish are harvested annually as well, an industry that has continued to grow even as fin fishing has ebbed.

It's also a very pretty place.

* * *

Enclosing Chatham's eastern shoreline is the long, thin strip of sand known formally as Nauset Beach, locally as North Beach. Originating about 10 miles to the north in the town of Orleans, Nauset is a barrier beach, an extension of the Great Outer Beach of Cape Cod. The cliffs of Truro, Wellfleet and Eastham are its parents, its siblings the Monomoy Islands which dangle off Chatham's south coast. The name North Beach was first applied to the peninsula to distinguish the main portion of Nauset from the periodically isolated south island, or South Beach; it also emerged from the fact that the point of the beach always progresses from north to south after a major breach. Among locals, though the charts and maps may say Nauset, it is always North Beach.

The summer before the breakthrough, I made my first trip to the outer beach, accessible only by boat or four-wheel drive vehicle from the parking lot of spectacular Nauset Beach in Orleans.

What I found was a sparse, slightly anachronistic landscape, a place apart from the sound and fury across Chatham Harbor. I stayed at one of 40 or so cottages, which are called camps by the occupants, since many of them were originally hunting camps. They are grouped in two distinct "villages." We had to work a hand pump to get a drink of water or to wash. No telephones; a few camps have generators, some have gas-powered appliances, but most function without modern amenities, just as they have for decades. And I had my first experience with an outhouse.

On North Beach, even the minor annoyances of life in Chatham melt away just as quickly as an ice cream cone under the blazing August sun. It is the most quiet place within the bounds of Chatham, where the noises of nature dominate. They aren't really noises at all, though, but a kind of music: wind and birds singing a counterpoint melody to the incessant rhythm of the sea's pounding percussion. At night, the roar of the waves on the outer beach fills the air like thunder.

So far removed is life on North Beach that the town, often seen across the harbor through a hazy mist of low-lying fog, seems like a picture, a projection, perhaps an illusion. Yet it provides a backdrop of eerie beauty: sunsets behind Chatham cast an ethereal glow over the town and drape the beach's low dunes and scrub growth in a chiaroscuro cloak cut only by the brilliant blade of light thrown seaward by the Chatham Lighthouse. Herons, gulls and terns shrouded in darkness stand out against backlighting that almost make you believe life can sometimes be like the movies.

* * *

After writing countless articles on the North Beach break and its effects for The Cape Cod Chronicle, listening to hours of discussion in endless meetings and hearings, taking hundreds of photographs of erosion-sculpted dunes, crashing waves and devastated ocean-front cottages, I started thinking: There's a story here.

But more than just a series of news stories strung together, it is a true natural and social history, a classic study of man versus nature. The scientific principles of the Nauset barrier beach cycle were well-understood, but with the excitement and near-hysteria following the 1987 breach and subsequent erosion, it wasn't being viewed with any sort of perspective, scientific or historical. We knew the beach had broken through and the shore had eroded in the past. Any Chatham native will tell you it was inevitable, that his or her parents and grandparents watched helplessly a hundred years ago as the ocean poured through a break in almost exactly the same spot as the present one and claimed two lighthouses and numerous homes.

So I did some research, talked to historians, scientists, property owners and old timers, and put together this story of North Beach and its relationship to the town and people of Chatham, from the first set-

tlers to the recent court battles over the rights of private property owners to protect their land from nature with rocks and stones. It isn't
meant to be a comprehensive, authoritative history. Rather, it should
be read as a chronicle of nature's unceasing challenge to man, at once
beyond our reach and yet very, very close to home.

By 1992, South Beach had attached to Lighthouse Beach, making accessible
one of the Cape's most beautiful barrier beaches.

THE STORY OF CHATHAM'S NORTH BEACH

NATURE'S DESIGN: THE
BARRIER BEACH CYCLE

On a clear day, the view from the lookout at the Chatham Lighthouse Beach overlook reaches to the almost indiscernible thread-like line where ocean meets sky, where never-ending blue hovers above darkly reflective water, cut occasionally by the ghostly whitecap of a wave or the hazy outline of a passing ship. It's one of the most spectacular views on Cape Cod.

Nowadays, though, eyes seldom stray much beyond the scene that lies just off Lighthouse Beach. The Atlantic waters churn and roil as the tide ebbs and flows through a two-mile-wide inlet, hypnotizing, furious, beautiful. Nauset Beach — North Beach after it crosses the Chatham town line — once stretched clear across what is now open water, something people visiting the overlook for the first time often find difficult to believe. But through a process as old as Cape Cod, the barrier beach has been violated, ravaged by nature. And still it appears, to the observer leaning against the ever-present clammy breeze 35 feet above the beach, to remain in the grip of nature's chaotic fury.

But there is order here. Every wave has its purpose, every tidal flat straggling off the southern tip of North Beach like a mini-archipelago fits into the scheme of the barrier beach cycle.

First described in detail by Professor Henry Mitchell in an 1874 report to the U.S. Harbor Commission, the Chatham barrier beach cycle consists of a 100- to 150-year-long process of beach construction and destruction, of migrating inlets and catastrophic erosion, illustrative of nature's power, logic and consistency. It's also a story inexorably linked to Chatham and its people, whose homes and livelihoods have over the years been at once dependent upon, and at the mercy of, the beach and the sea.

To understand the relationship between Chatham and the beach, it's necessary to look first at the geology and geological processes underlying Cape Cod as a whole, and the barrier beach system in particular.

As you stand at the Chatham Lighthouse breathing the salty ocean air and drinking in nature's handiwork, imagine yourself 40 miles to the east. Around you the dark ocean swells and dips, the only sounds the piercing scream of the gulls and the wet slap of sea against hull. If you sever Cape Cod from Massachusetts and make it disappear, the spot where you stood, with the lighthouse behind you, would be equally wet and lonely. The peninsula of Cape Cod juts 40 miles eastward into the Atlantic from the continental United States, taking a radical 90-degree turn northward at Chatham, and continuing another 35 miles or so to Wood's End, at the tip of Provincetown.

Which leaves Chatham, at the Cape's elbow, "a veritable town at sea, lying farther oceanward than any other town in the United States," observed Chatham native George "Chart" Eldridge, the 19th century hydrographer who founded the Eldridge Tide Charts, on which mariners have relied for more than a century. While there are points in Maine that are farther east than Chatham, no single community, not even our southern neighbor Nantucket, reaches as far, as tentatively, into the waiting arms of the Atlantic.

And embrace Chatham the ocean does, surrounding it on three sides with waters of different temperaments and personalities. To the south, Nantucket Sound's warm, gentle fingers caress the shoreline of West and South Chatham; to the north, the 7,285-acre Pleasant Bay, one of the largest, most productive and fragile estuaries in Massachusetts, and the Muddy Creek inlet enclose Eastward Point and Chathamport; flanking the eastern shoreline from North Chatham to Morris Island is Chatham Harbor; and just beyond the narrow spit of North Beach, the cold Atlantic.

Chatham was left in this precarious position after the ice sheets of the Wisconsin glacier retreated about 15,000 years ago. Before that, Chatham and the rest of the Cape had, for millions of years, been part of the northern edge of the exposed Atlantic Coastal Plain, now the submerged Continental Shelf, once an expanse of low-lying land which extended some 200 miles east of what is now the Outer Cape. During the Pleistocene Epoch, vast glaciers, more than a mile thick in places and originating in what is now Labrador, slid down to cover much of North America, carrying with them mineral debris dredged up along the way. After thousands of years the climate began to warm, and the glaciers retreated, carving furrows in the landscape and depositing their cargo of rock and sand and soil as they went.

The melting glaciers formed three ice bodies over what was to become Cape Cod: the Buzzard's Bay, Cape Cod Bay and South Channel Lobes. The Cape Cod Bay Lobe, to the north of Chatham, and the South Channel Lobe, to the east, left behind two deposits known as the Harwich and Nauset Heights outwash plains. Outwash is distinguished from the hilly boulder and gravel moraine deposits left by glaciers to the north and west, also referred to as glacial till, by its gently sloping, structured terrain composed mostly of gravelly sand. It is these glacial deposits, sculpted atop the older clay and rock of the coastal plain, which form the hooked, bent-arm landscape of Cape Cod. (The distinction between outwash and moraine becomes important later on in this story in determining the applicability of state laws prohibiting seawalls on dunes, i.e., outwash).

The area's numerous kettle ponds, bays and inlets were formed by stranded glaciers which melted in pits and furrows left by the retreating ice. As the glaciers melted, there was a corresponding rise in sea level (some 400 feet in 14,000 years), which filled the remaining gashes in the landscape, creating the inner shoreline. Wind, ocean waves and currents, in turn, ate away the newborn upland. Those forces, 3,000 to 4,000 years ago, created the Cape's major sand spits and dunes: the Province Lands, Sandy Neck, Monomoy and Nauset.

Which brings us, in geological terms, into the present. The smooth convex curve of Nauset/North Beach, when in one piece, extends at its longest 14 miles from Orleans to Chatham; Monomoy, the system's southern extreme, continues another eight miles. At times, the two have been connected. Usually, that happens after a breach in the barrier beach to the north, so that there is rarely, if ever, one continuous beach from Orleans to the southern tip of Monomoy.

As a barrier beach, North Beach shelters Chatham's mainland from the ocean's direct force, creating a stable inner shoreline and a relatively safe and calm navigable deep-water harbor. Barrier beaches are common throughout the eastern United States and are defined as low sand dunes separated from the main coast by a body of water. They take on various configurations: A barrier spit is joined to the mainland at one end (in rare cases, both ends), like North Beach in its most familiar form; a barrier island, as its name implies, is not connected to the main shore at all. Perhaps the best known barrier beach is Cape Hatteras, in North Carolina, a 180-mile-long series of barrier islands and spits running the length of that state's coast. Various barrier beaches can be found on the Cape and Islands, including Sandy Neck in Sandwich and Barnstable and Great Island in Wellfleet, though the Nauset system is by far the largest and most dynamic.

Whatever their shape, barrier beaches are by definition unstable, shifting land forms dependent on the wind and tide for their sustaining component, sand. The Nauset system looks 25 miles north to the imposing coastal cliffs of Truro, Wellfleet and Eastham for the sediment that feeds it, transported by wave and tidal current action (littoral drift is the scientific term) and deposited, like a sculptor applying layer after layer of clay, at the southernmost tip of the barrier beach.

The erosion rate of those cliffs is well-documented. When it was built in South Wellfleet in 1901, the transmitting and receiving station from which Guglielmo Marconi sent the first wireless trans-Atlantic message stood more than 300 feet east of the present shoreline, where there is now only the churning waters of the Atlantic. Erosion forced the station's relocation, in 1914, to a more stable location near Ryder's Cove in Chatham. At Truro's Highland Light, wind and wave action carves out about three feet of upland a year, and at Nauset Beach in Eastham, the shoreline recedes at a rate greater than five feet annually. At both those locations, massive public works projects were necessary in the mid-1990s to move both the Nauset Lighthouse and the Highland Light back from the shore due to encroaching erosion. But Truro, Eastham and Wellfleet's loss is North Beach's gain. Victor Goldsmith, in his 1972 doctoral dissertation on the Nauset system, wrote that the Outer Cape constitutes "one of the largest known volumes of sediment transported by longshore drift." Dr. Graham Giese, in his 1978 report on the barrier beach, put the amount of sand carved from the cliffs and carried southward at 300,000 cubic yards per year; a lot of sand, enough to fill a dozen football fields 15 feet high. This translates to a growth rate for North Beach of about two miles every 20 years as sand is deposited at the beach's terminus.

At the same time, other, less visible forces are at work on the beach. Coastal submergence is the term used to describe the increase in sea level relative to the mainland, which is actually sinking due to gravity and other pressures. Submergence shapes the contours of the shoreline — both on the inner and outer beaches — and even a slight increase in the rate of the ocean's rise can have a drastic effect on the coast. In his report, Dr. Giese cited a sea level increase of between .005 and .01 feet per year, resulting in one-quarter to one-eighth of an acre of upland being lost to the ocean for every linear mile of coast.

Estimates of the rate of sea level rise have been revised upwards in the years since Dr. Giese wrote his report. The Greenhouse Effect — the warming of the Earth's temperature due to the introduction of synthetic compounds, man-made gases and chemicals into the atmosphere — is considered the major culprit; the compounds trap the planet's radiant heat, hastening the melting of our old friends, the glaciers, now relegated to the extreme north and south poles. Although the Greenhouse Effect theory remains controversial and is not universally accepted, estimates of the sea's increasing levels range from .45 feet to 1.57 feet per year; the latter figure, a "worst case" scenario presented in a Commonwealth of Massachusetts report in 1987, would consume 3.11 percent of Chatham's upland annually, cause massive erosion and drastic changes in marine habitats. In real terms, sea level rise has yet to make much of an impact on New England, yet the results of the 1987 breakthrough in Chatham, which created higher tides and more opportunity for storm damage, provided a glimpse of a potentially devastating future.

The triad of factors controlling North Beach's shape, then, are coastal submergence, sea level rise, and wave and tidal action. Now we know what the beach is, how it got here, and what forces are at work on it; how do these factors mesh to create a regular cycle of beach growth, breaching, disintegration and regrowth?

At both the beginning and end of the cycle, North Beach is one continuous stretch of sand, extending southerly from Orleans, enveloping Pleasant Bay and Chatham, as it was before the 1987 breach, and as historical maps show it was in 1846. Once the southern end of the beach begins to overlap Monomoy, the tidal flow in and out of Chatham Harbor and Pleasant Bay becomes constricted; it's like four lanes of traffic suddenly narrowing to one. Anyone who has drive down Route 6 in Dennis at the height of the summer season knows that means gridlock. The same thing happens to tidal flow. The estuary's resources wane and water stagnates as the tidal flow ebbs before an adequate amount of water can be exchanged between ocean and bay. Tidal ranges between the inner and outer beaches draw farther apart; the ocean side stands at about six to seven feet, the harbor and bay nearly three and a half. There is about a two-hour lag between high and low tide on either side of the barrier beach. Treacherous shoals and bars, infamous off Chatham for centuries, develop at the mouth of the harbor, known as the South Way in the latter stages of the cycle.

With the stage set thus, the time is right for a breach. Now, as Professor Mitchell noted, "the too confined waters of Pleasant Bay force a more direct outlet again, and the march of the beach from above has recommenced."

It's like squeezing a tube of toothpaste with the cap still on. The material under pressure has to go someplace. In the case of North Beach, a new inlet is created in the place of least resistance; historically, this has been opposite Minister's (Allen's) Point. Factors must be right for a permanent break to occur: usually a high pressure weather system, which drains the bay and harbor to lower-than-normal levels, a strong northeast storm and higher-than-normal tides. All of these were present when the beach broke in January 1987.

The location of the most recent break was somewhat unexpected; inlets had formed east of Minister's Point in the 17th, 18th and 19th centuries, according to a study by geologist Charles E. McClennen. Even Dr. Giese, in his 1978 report, projected a late 20th century breakthrough opposite Minister's Point. Nature, defying predictions as always, stole south in 1987 when nobody was looking and punched a hole through the beach directly opposite the Chatham Lighthouse.

When a breach is wide and deep and permanent enough, the differences in the hydrological pressure between the harbor and the ocean speed the tidal exchange through the new inlet, scour it and keep it open, all the time battling the southern littoral drift which naturally wants to plug the hole up again. The velocity of the current instead sweeps sediment into the harbor, plugging that up, much to the consternation of fishermen and recreational boaters. Literally starved of sand, the southern portion of the beach (South Beach in local parlance), now an island off and on connected to the mainland, gradually over a period of decades is eroded and overwashed westward, filling up the inner harbor with shoals and flats and cutting off the old southern inlet. Eventually South Beach disappears, the sand migrating onto the mainland, Morris Island, and the northern end of Monomoy. North Beach's southern tip then slowly begins to grow southward.

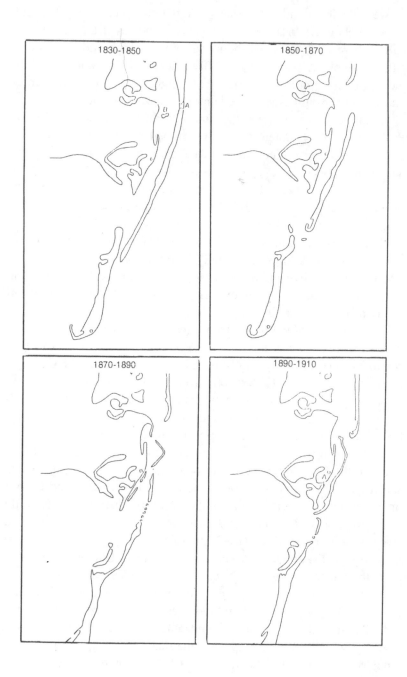

BREAKTHROUGH

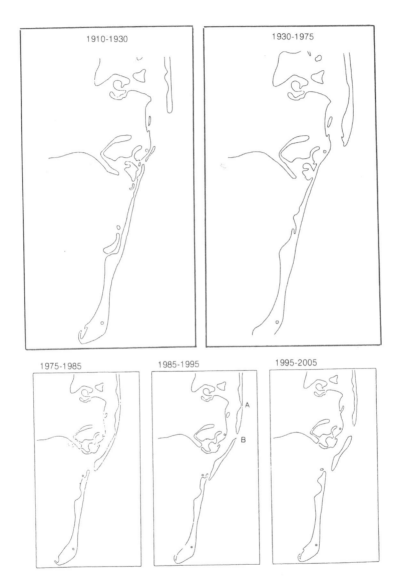

PREDICTIONS OF MOVEMENT OF THE NORTH BEACH BARRIER SYSTEM, AS WELL AS HISTORICAL COMPOSITES, AS PUBLISHED IN DR. GRAHAM GIESE'S 1978 REPORT. "A" ON THE CENTER DIAGRAM ABOVE MARKS THE LOCATION OF THE 1946 BREACH; "B" IS THE 1987 BREAKTHROUGH.

THE STORY OF CHATHAM'S NORTH BEACH 19

Then the cycle starts all over again.

No doubt this has been happening for thousands of years, but reliable maps and records documenting the process go back only two centuries. A permanent break in the making was first viewed by eyewitnesses in 1846; previous to that the harbor had become so choked and constricted with shoals that it threatened to ruin Chatham's seafaring economy. In 1841, Edward Hitchcock noted that 20 years earlier, Chatham's harbor was excellent; but two decades later it had filled in. "Nothing can save it from complete destruction," he wrote, "but forming a new entrance."

The U.S. Army Corps of Engineers would use almost the same language in a 1968 report on the feasibility of cutting a new inlet in North Beach. "Daily tidal delays [have] become common to the commercial fishing boats as well as a threat to life," the report stated, concluding that "if no navigational improvements are made in the area, it is expected that the existing Chatham Harbor inlet will in the not too distant future close completely." (The corps' report is explored in depth in Chapter Two.)

The area was first mapped by English navigator Bartholomew Gosnold in 1602. From descriptions of his sightings in W. Sears Nickerson's *Land Ho!* and elsewhere, it appears that at the time, North Beach had been breached some years before and was well into the inlet migration cycle. The land he named Gilbert Point was attached to the mainland at approximately the present day location of Minister's Point, and curved south and east to a point opposite the present day lighthouse. In 1606, Samuel De Champlain produced a map describing a spit that terminated more to the south. Records of Sutcliffe's Inlet of 1619, which opened into Pleasant Bay east of Strong Island, and Governor William Bradford's 1622 entrance north of that seem to indicate that the beach was in the process of breaking up, with washovers and inlets forming up and down its length.

Since 1620, Goldsmith noted, North Beach has undergone "at least two, probably three full cycles of the large scale inlet migration." From the maps and descriptions extant, it seems likely that a major breach occurred sometime prior to Gosnold's visit in 1602, probably opposite Minister's Point. The severed southern portion of the broken beach attached itself to North Chatham, as if the mainland had grown an arm, and gradually welded onto the shoreline. Des Barres put the entrance to "Old Harbor" just north of Minister's Point in 1740; the beach built

BREAKTHROUGH

steadily south from there until the next major breach, in 1846. The 1740 entrance probably marked the spot of another major breakthrough. Will this process continue for thousands of years to come? Dr. Giese doesn't think so.

He noted in his report that like the cliffs to the north, Nauset/North Beach is also moving westward year by year, an important factor when it comes to restricting the flow of water in and out of Pleasant Bay, Sand is moved from the east side of the barrier beach to the west by winds and storm washovers, and it is also deposited along the inner beach as flood tidal deltas. According to Giese, the entire beach shifts west at a rate of between five and 10 feet a year.

Perhaps the most dramatic demonstration of the beach's constant desire to "go west" is the case of the Sparrow Hawk. The ship either piled up on shoals or was wrecked in the night, according to William Bradford, on the inner shore of Nauset Beach just south of Hog Island in greater Pleasant Bay in 1626. The wreck was discovered 237 years later when erosion on the *outer* shore uncovered the wooden remains. During the intervening years, the beach had moved west a distance approximately equal to its width, about 1,000 feet, right over the wrecked ship.

Giese theorizes that after several more cycles, the northernmost portion of North Beach will have migrated so far west that it will "no longer overlap the mainland of Chatham. Rather, the barrier beach system will stop at North Chatham, the coast from North Chatham to Morris Island will be exposed to ocean waves and an ever-widening barrier spit will extend southward from Morris Island."

Which means that, about 500 years from today, the open-ocean exposure and tremendous erosion Chatham's eastern shoreline has experienced in recent times could be status quo. That probably wouldn't have surprised our forefathers. They might not have had the scientific understanding of the barrier beach cycle we have today, but when devastation came, when lighthouses tumbled into the sea and waves lapped at doorsteps, they didn't complain or attempt to fight back against nature. They took it in stride, built new lighthouses away from the sea cliffs and moved their homes inland. In some innate way, born, probably, of their close association with the sea, they understood and accepted the powerful, unseen hands that constantly mold the beach. That appreciation seems lost today.

* * *

In April 1988, after more than a year of observations, Dr. Giese came up with a few revised theories about the North Beach barrier beach system. There appeared to be three separate and distinct phases to the process: first, the switch in emphasis from the southern inlet to the new cut, which happened much quicker than expected; after just over a year, Dr. Giese estimated 90 percent of the tidal exchange between the Chatham Harbor/Pleasant Bay system and the ocean flowed through the break.

We are now in the midst of the second phase, the breaking up of South Beach. For the past several years, a bridge of sand has connected the beach to the mainland just south of Lighthouse Beach. In a recent study, scientists predicted that in a matter of years, all of the sand between South Beach and the mainland will be gone, washed onto the mainland or lost to the deep water. Starved of sand, South Beach's dunes are getting lower and lower. In a slow process that could take up to 50 years, overwashes will lower the beach even more, and it will begin to break up, the sand drifting southwesterly and possibly melding onto the mainland from the Morris Island dike south. A large salt marsh would be lost, but ironically the sand could protect dozens of homes lying between Little Beach and Morris Island Road, and Morris Island itself, from devastating erosion. Chatham's eastern shoreline would then look much as it did some 50 years ago, with a clear path lying ahead of North Beach as it begins the third and final phase of the process: building south once more toward the next inevitable breakthrough.

THE BREAK, 1988.

BREAKTHROUGH

THE GREAT BEACH

Chatham is at war with the Atlantic.
— J. CLINTON HAMMOND, DECEMBER 1987

November 15, 1871. Dark, angry skies dulled the morning dawning over Chatham. Winds whipped around from the northeast. Fishermen, seeing what was coming in the heavy, portentous clouds, made fast their boats. The lighthouse keeper maintained a vigilant watch for vessels in trouble as winds grew to gale force, rains descended and the tide rose to the highest level in 15 years.

It is not recorded what time of day it happened, but sometime during that raging easterly, "the most terrific storm since 1851," in the words of *Chatham Monitor* editor D.B. Gifford, North Beach was "torn asunder" directly across the harbor from the twin lights, sending land-hungry waves crashing around the pilings of Hardy's wharf, at the foot of the bluff.

Although a breakthrough had formed an inlet east of Minister's Point in 1846, it was the 1871 breach that hit Chatham hard — at least as hard as 1987's breach and in approximately the same location. Eager to have at the shoreline, the Atlantic began a relentless siege that spanned the next decade, not only robbing Chatham of homes and property, but also stealing the foundations out from under its venerable twin lights.

Fortunately for passing mariners, who depended upon the lights' beacons to guide them around the punishing shoals to the southeast, the government had the foresight — and the time — to build a new set of lights before the old ones were claimed by the sea. But from the time of that fateful storm, when the brick towers stood 228 feet from the edge of the bank, until their surrender eight years later, Chatham's citizens held a tense vigil the likes of which would not be repeated for more than a century.

The first records we have of the Nauset barrier beach's breaking through date to the 1846 breach, which initiated the cycle that ended with the January 1987 breakthrough, according to Dr. Graham Giese. There are nautical charts going back to 1602 that place inlets in various locations up and down the sand spit, and even a few written descriptions and anecdotes about what the early settlers called "The Great Beach." But there is little else of substance on the historical record. One reason for this dearth of information is that it wasn't until 1819 that a white man claimed ownership of what we know today as North Beach. Monomoy, at the time considered part of "The Great Beach," had been parceled off almost 100 years earlier due to the value, as pasture land, of its lush salt meadows and fields of sedge grass.

What the Great Beach meant to the area's original inhabitants is open to speculation. Man appears to have lived on what is now Cape Cod since before the last ice age; by the time European settlers arrived, numerous tribes of Native Americans called the peninsula home. In Chatham, the native people were known as the Monomoyicks, a branch of the great Wampanoag nation that once ranged throughout southern New England. Theirs was an agricultural society; living by the sea, though, they did a fair share of fishing and shellfish harvesting, as excavations of ancient shell mounds, known as middens, have shown. Perhaps they saw the Great Beach as a protector, keeping the elemental force of the ocean at bay and providing easily accessible food; maybe it was, to them, simply the end of the land.

The identity of the first non-native to see the shores of Nauset Beach is also a question that will probably never be answered conclusively. The Vikings and Norsemen who ventured westward to fish the rich grounds off Nova Scotia in the Middle Ages may have traveled as far south as the Cape chasing abundant cod, but there are no reliable records or relics to prove this. A number of early explorers skirted the Cape's shores, but they didn't tell us much about the land they saw. It wasn't until Bartholomew Gosnold dubbed the peninsula "Cape Cod" in 1602 that we have a good indication of the lay of the land. According to W. Sears Nickerson's *Land Ho!*, Gosnold noted two inlets through the outer beach into Pleasant Bay in May of 1602. A spit of land lying to the south he named Gilbert's Point.

Four years later, on his second voyage to the area, French explorer Samuel De Champlain rounded that same point and, assured by the natives that a safe harbor lay ahead, fought a tense battle against the shoals and currents off Monomoy before swinging into what we now know as Stage Harbor. He called the place Port Fortune, landed, had a deadly scuffle with the Indians, and before leaving sketched a map generally believed to be the most accurate of its time.

By Champlain's map, and descriptions by other mariners exploring the coast during the next 20 years, we can reconstruct the North Beach of the time as somewhere in the middle of its 150-year cycle. Its appearance was very different from today's beach, cut-through and all. To the north, just east of Strong Island, a chunk of beach formed an island, separating Nauset to the north and the peninsula to the south by two entrances to the bay called Sutcliffe's Inlets by Englishman Thomas Dermer in 1619 (it was inside the northernmost of these inlets that the Sparrow Hawk was wrecked in 1626). The southern part of the beach was attached to the mainland at Minister's Point, curved back east and then south along its usual course, terminating approximately opposite Morris Island at Gosnold's Gilbert's Point. Enfolded by the beach was an island called Cotchpinicut by the natives, Ram Island by the Europeans; it appeared on charts until it was submerged during a violent storm in the early 1800s.

North Beach also has the auspicious honor of being the nearest land to the Mayflower during the Pilgrims' first night anchored off the shores of the New World. Today's Old Nauset Lifesaving Station in Eastham is the approximate point east of which William Bradford and company first sighted land on the morning of November 9, 1620. Sailing south, the intrepid band of Puritans turned back after narrowly escaping destruction on the shoals of Pollock Rip, and hovered overnight five to eight miles off Chatham before turning north and landing in Provincetown Harbor two days later. In his book detailing the journey, W. Sears Nickerson quotes an old mariner as saying that given the plethora of vessels that shoals off Chatham would eventually claim, "The Pilgrims never knew how near they came to settling on Monomoy Point."

Which would have made Chatham, Cape Cod and possibly all of New England somewhat different than today.

The Great Beach looked a bit different when William Nickerson struck a bargain with the Monomoyick sachem Mattaquason in 1656 and for the price of a boat and some trinkets, came into possession of the land that is Chatham today. Early sketches reproduced in William C. Smith's *History of Chatham* indicate the beach at the time (called the "Monomoit Great Beach") was a continuous spit, much as it was 300 years later. One of the later sketches, dated 1691-94, shows an inlet opposite Strong Island, the traditional location of Chatham's "Old Harbor."

William Nickerson, whose descendants still populate the area, was by all accounts a conscientious and law abiding Englishman. But his first purchase was held in violation of a law requiring that the Plymouth Colony Court approve all deals with natives. Thus he was forced to start again from square one. He petitioned the court for permission to purchase the tract he'd already, in effect, bought from Mattaquason, but was awarded only a portion. Through three subsequent purchases, for amounts ranging from 90 pounds to cattle and livestock, he obtained from other titleholders the whole of his original claim. From approximately Oyster Pond east, however, the land remained in Monomoyick hands and was known as the Indian Grounds. It included the Great Beach.

Originally attached to the settlement at Yarmouth, where Nickerson had lived, and still later to the parish at Eastham (communities in those days were generally organized around churches, the social and political focus for the early settlers), Monomoy, as the area was known, became a separate constablewick in 1679. Smith describes the early settlers, overwhelmingly Nickerson's relatives and offspring, as farmers who lived near the shore for convenient access to abundant shell and fin fish. They also appeared to have pursued whales, on a small scale; Smith writes that there was a "substantial whale boat owned in the village at an early date, the citizens holding it in shares."

That early vessel may well have been the beginning of what would grow to become one of the Cape's largest commercial fishing fleets. For more than a century Chatham sent ships and sailors to all corners of the globe, while local fishermen, who seldom strayed beyond Georges Bank in their quest for plentiful groundfish and other species, made the town a progressively important fishing port, an industry that continues today.

In their 1711 incorporation petition to the General Court of Massachusetts, the five selectmen (including three Nickersons; a descendant remains on the board today) of the village of Monomoy made sure to point out how the town had been "heretofore a place of relief to many ship wrecked vessels & Englishmen cast ashore in storms upon the beech of Sandy Poynt [the tip of North Beach] or Rack Cove [Monomoy Island]," and how "likewise it has the most pleasant situation & incomparable conveniency for most sorts of fishery." Their petition was granted, and on June 11, 1712, "Monomoy" was scratched off the map and "Chatham" written in (the town was named for Chatham, England, an important naval port at the mouth of the Medway River on Britain's east coast).

In the early years of the settlement, the Great Beach — an appellation generally applied to both Nauset/North Beach and Monomoy (on and off one continuous sand spit) — was used as a grazing land for horses and cattle, according to Smith. The livestock could be herded out onto the beach's low-lying meadows and salt marshes where it attached to the mainland at Chathamport, and from there they had the range of the beach, extending five or six miles to Monomoy. This eventually caused problems among the residents, apparently, and in 1691 a group of settlers petitioned the Great Court for permission to purchase the entire beach. Smith reports that no action was taken, since the land was reserved for the "old comers," those originally assigned purchasing rights to the lower Cape by the Plymouth Court (from whom William Nickerson purchased most of his Chatham lands).

The descendants of the "old comers" didn't assert their rights to purchase the beach until 1711, when they bought "all the meadow and sedge ground" from Sipson's bound (Strong Island) south from the local Monomoyicks. They began dividing up the beach, but ran into trouble with two other groups who also claimed the purchase rights. The dispute continued for some years until, according to Smith, there was "some kind of lawsuit" in 1724 which established the Nickerson family as the legitimate owners of the Great Beach. "When this question had been finally settled," Smith writes, "the parties came together and agreed upon an equal division of the beach between them."

Attention was principally centered on Monomoy, which was wider than North Beach and richer in meadow and sedge land. William Eldredge built a house and opened a tavern on Monomoy Island in 1711. Over the years, a small, deep-water inlet known as the Powder Hole became a popular harbor of refuge (it is now little more than a shallow, brackish mudhole). Eventually, a settlement called Whitewash

Village sprang up. It included a school and numerous homes, all centered around the Monomoy lighthouse, but gradually died off as the Powder Hole filled in. Monomoy, however, is another story for another time, its history rich but brief and its fate only indirectly linked to North Beach.

Nobody seems to have bothered too much about North Beach at the time. The valuable salt meadows were for the most part located south of Morris Island, so "no other part was then considered to be of any value," according to Smith. Not until nearly 100 years later, in 1819, did the descendants of the original owners think to do anything about the northern part of the Great Beach. No doubt, the beach's ephemeral nature, its combination of low rolling dunes and sparse beach grass, and its narrow width made it seem not worth bothering about.

As noted previously, an inlet, at the traditional location of Old Harbor, appeared north of Minister's Point circa 1740. The beach probably extended a bit south from that point, but not very far. If the pattern is consistent, during the late 1700s the remaining south beach moved westward, attaching to the mainland. The owners probably had little interest then in land that was disappearing before their very eyes. Some maps indicate during the latter part of the 18th century a spit extended from James' Head, the original name for the bluff where the Chatham Lighthouse is located, south to Monomoy (not unlike today's South Beach). In the following years, the beach built southward until, by 1819, the beach had restored itself to nearly its full length, and the owners had something they could sell. Whatever the motive, Smith's book states that the remaining Great Beach was auctioned to the highest bidders in three lots. Names of the new owners included Nickerson, Young, Doane, Atwood, Howes, Crowell and Sears, some of which still appear on today's list of Chatham residents and North Beach property owners.

By that time Chatham had grown into quite a vital community. The population increased 129 percent between 1775 and 1830, when 2,130 people lived in town. Maritime activities were quickly outpacing farming as the economy's mainstay, but not without the threat of difficulties. North Beach's point, by 1825, extended a bit south of Morris Island. The trip from the Old Harbor to the ocean was long and difficult over tricky shoals and continually shifting sand bars. As the inlet to the Atlantic migrated southward, so did the village center. The area known today as the Old Village — basically lower Main Street

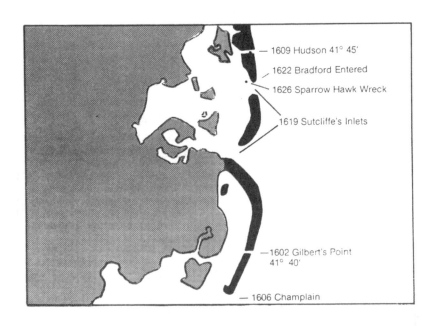

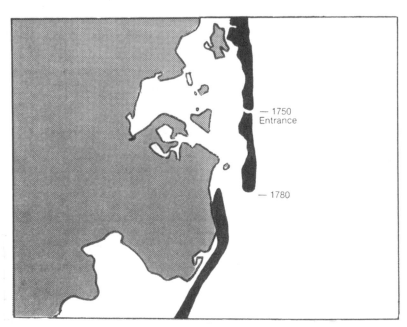

NAUSET SPIT CHANGES INTHE 18TH CENTURY (BASED ON USGS 1873 REPORT; NICKERSON, 1930).

THE STORY OF CHATHAM'S NORTH BEACH

from Chatham Bars Avenue to the Coast Guard station — built up around the wharves of the neighborhood called Scrabbletown and twin wooden lighthouses constructed on the James' Head bluff in 1808.

At a town meeting on June 30, 1831, the citizens of Chatham established a committee to inspect the Old Harbor area and determine what improvements, if any, could be made to navigation. The following February the committee made its report: The best approach to rejuvenate Old Harbor and make passage safer for vessels was to follow the lead of Hyannis and build a canal and breakwater through the outer beach.

Seven years previously, the original 300-yard Hyannis breakwater, one of the first waterways projects built with funds appropriated by the United States Congress, had elevated that village to one of the busiest ports on the Cape, second only to Provincetown. That obviously had an impact on certain "wealthy men," owners of vessels based in Old Harbor, who appear to have been the driving force behind the Nauset Beach canal, according to an article detailing the project's history in the December 9, 1875, issue of the *Chatham Monitor*.

Even though the majority of voters backed the project, a subsequent vote in March of 1832 reveals a skepticism that may be part Yankee realism, part natural distrust of anything that interfered with Mother Nature. Nathan Crosby, who formed the Truro Breakwater Company to take on the canal job, would be paid $4,000 for the work, but only if it was successful; success was defined as the canal staying open for at least six months.

Scrabbletowners "naturally took umbrage" to the plan, which would return the town's economic focus to Old Harbor. Resenting what would be both an economic and social loss to the village, they ridiculed the project and made up scurrilous poems about the Harwich and Orleans men hired to dig the canal, according to the *Monitor*.

They had little to fear. Although the canal was apparently completed, local historian Joseph Nickerson (a tenth generation descendant of Chatham's founder) says sediment and sand drifting south quickly filled it in.

Noted *Monitor* editor Levi Atwood in 1875, 40 years later, as Chatham's eastern shoreline shook under the unceasing pounding of the ocean, "For the past few years, the town has had no occasion to dig canals, Old Neptune giving them all they need."

Atwood (the town clerk, treasurer, Sunday school teacher and merchant who took over the local paper's editorship from D.B. Gifford) was referring to the series of washovers and breaches begun with the formation, in 1846, of a new inlet opposite Minister's Point. This was the first recorded break in Nauset Beach during the modern era; as noted by Giese, Goldsmith and the Army Corps of Engineers, the Great Beach had been unbroken (except for the aborted canal and occasional temporary washovers) for the previous 20 years, and had advanced two miles south during that time.

The position of North Beach in the months just before the 1846 breach was nearly identical to its configuration in the latter days of 1986.

The specific conditions that engendered the 1846 breach aren't recorded. What is clear, however, is that the new South Beach began to fall apart soon after, hastened by a series of severe storms. A northeaster in 1851, known as Minot's Gale, ripped an 800-foot wide swath in the beach that soon scoured to sufficient depth so that boats with drafts of more than 10 feet could pass through unhindered, which took some gutsy sailing. Even with today's modern navigational technology, it takes skill to maneuver through the present cut.

The same gale wiped from sight Ram Island; a subsequent hurricane in 1869 caused more damage. In 1847, a United States Coastal and Geodetic Survey team took their first profiles of Nauset Beach. Between that year and 1868, 11.4 acres of beach disappeared annually, a total loss of some 239 acres. During the same period, the northern tip of South Beach curved westward more than 2,800 feet. Throughout these years, most of the mainland remained untouched by the changes, or, at least, nothing catastrophic occurred in the way of erosion or property damage. If land was washed away, no one's house went with it, that much is certain. The changes in tidal regimes and water temperature seem to have been, at most, of passing concern. At least until the easterly of November 15, 1871, which laid open the village's vulnerable belly and changed forever the shape of the inner harbor.

The bluff at James' Head was then some 40 to 50 feet above the beach, and extended almost 500 feet east of the present lighthouse and Coast Guard station. Land to the immediate north stretched about that same distance east from the present dune line. Water Street ended as far east as Holway Street did prior to the 1987 break; a row of houses sat below the bluff, just west of the wharves.

The storm was the most severe to hit this coast since Minot's Gale.

In the edition following the storm, *Monitor* editor Gifford wrote:

"Twenty years ago [1851] that part of the beach upon which the security of the harbor at North Chatham depended was destroyed; and ever since, by the continual action of ocean, the beach has gradually narrowed till it was unable to withstand the fearful sea which was driven against it during the recent gale. Forty years ago it was at least one-half mile wide at that part which lies opposite Captain Josiah Hardy's wharf, and quite an elevated crest ran alone its entire length; but now for the space of an eighth of a mile in length the sea, at high water, completely covers it."

Gifford, at least, recognized the powerful forces at work. "This beach has been the plaything of the Old Ocean for many a year," he wrote, "and its complete history would make an interesting chapter in the annals of the town. We should not be obliged to go back to geologic ages either to appreciate the vast changes which have taken place in its structure." The editor went on to make a dire prediction, bold for its time: "Eventually the remaining part [of the beach] will be removed and then the tide will begin to gnaw away at our very feet."

There was a bright side, though. Edward Hitchcock had, in 1841, mourned the loss of what had been an excellent port at Old Harbor. The 1846 breach began the Old Harbor's rehabilitation; but the 1871 breach shifted the emphasis south once again, creating, in Gifford's words, "a new harbor" for the village, where "there is abundant water now to float almost any craft...The prospect is good for a considerable improvement in business. It will make a good port and safe retreat for the fishermen in the fall, and open extensive resources for enterprising citizens."

Scrabbletown, it seemed, was saved.

It would be several years before the people of Chatham realized the cost of this new, improved harbor. During the next decade, "That Old Ocean" would more than exceed Gifford's prognostication, exacting a tribute that would include many acres of land, numerous homes and two lighthouses.

In 1872 and again the following year, more government surveys of the beach were taken. In that first year, 51.1 acres disappeared and the beach, both to the north and south, continued to narrow. (Remarking on the surveyor's visits, Gifford quipped in the November 13, 1873, *Monitor* that "the old Ocean has been playing such pranks with that venerable strip of land as would keep whole corps of the service busy

BREAKTHROUGH

noting its changes.")

Henry Mitchell, in his 1874 report to the U.S. Harbor Commission, noted, however, that "the upland has been but little disturbed during the past year, but attacks from the sea are so much apprehended, that buildings have been moved back from places where inroads were threatened." Chatham was preparing.

Moving a house in those days wasn't the major event it is today. Especially those houses along the shore; they were for the most part smallish Capes and shacks, with nothing as an anchor except, in some cases, a dank Cape Cod cellar. There is no telling how many buildings were moved during the decade following the 1871 breach, but those familiar with the village claim that today, many of the houses along lower Main Street and the other avenues of the Old Village once sat much closer to the shore.

By all accounts, the erosion was systematic but relatively slow. Houses did not fall into the sea after only a year, as in the late 1980s; but it wasn't long before results were as dramatic as anything seen in recent years. *The Monitor* noted in April 1875 that village residents watched the sea's eager encroachment "with no little anxiety."

"Where one year ago gardens were plowed and planted and crops grew, today a sea is breaking and foaming in all its fury and grandeur. The whole row of dwellings, buildings and stores along the margin of the harbor has been removed and, according to the present appearance, others still farther inland will have to share the same fate."

Since the construction of the first set of lighthouses on James' Head in 1808, the twin beacons had been a landmark for both mariners and landlubbers, as well as a symbol of the town. In 1840, the wooden structures were replaced by new brick lighthouse towers.

Josiah Hardy, a former sea captain, became the fourth lighthouse keeper of the new lights in December 1872, living in the adjacent keeper's house with his wife. Like many in the lighthouse service, Hardy kept a detailed account of activities during his 28-year tenure as keeper. Along with notations on storms, passing vessels, all-too-common wrecks, events of importance to the community ("January 12, 1873: Stephen Ellises house was burned down in the night") and general observances ("January 28th: Some 13 Blackfish was found Dead on the Beach & Bars."), Hardy kept a close watch on the eroding bluff, and it is his measurements that provide the most graphic picture of one of the most dramatic periods in the history of Chatham's interaction with North

Beach.

When he took over as keeper, the towers stood 228 feet from the edge of the bank. By December 1874, 38 feet had been carved away. Two years later, in an entry dated November 15, 1876 — the anniversary of the 1871 breach — Hardy noted that another northeast storm had caused further damage. The ocean, at that time, was stealing an average of 31 feet a year from the bluff as well as the low dunes farther south.

By February 1877, the south tower was 95 feet from the bluff's edge. As we've seen by Mitchell's report, the federal government was keeping a sharp eye on the situation at the Cape's elbow. On the 17th of February, a Mr. Lunt of the Harbor Commission visited the station to "witness the washing away of the shore line." In late April, the aptly-named Frederick Tower, an assistant engineer with the Lighthouse Board, arrived in town to begin survey work. On May 3, the *Monitor* reported the news: The government had approved the construction of a new set of lights and a keeper's house. The commission had concluded that it was not feasible to relocate the old towers, and assuring protection from almost certain destruction was impossible. Construction would begin immediately, "for fear [the old towers] may tumble over the precipice at no distant day."

Ground was broken on May 31 about 200 feet west of the old towers, on the mainland side of Main Street. The new north tower was completed on August 13, the south tower seven days later. They were lighted for the first time on September 6. And none too soon, Hardy's granddaughter, Grace, wrote in a history of the lighthouses published in 1924. "For the land was falling away fast," her pamphlet reads, "and Grandmother from her kitchen window and Grandfather from the towers could look almost directly down into the sea, only 77 feet now from the foot of the south tower."

The erosion was by then attracting sightseers. Chatham was a burgeoning summer resort, and the lighthouse work, as well as the work of nature, drew many curious visitors in their surreys and horsedrawn carriages. The view from the bluff was, as it is today, "truly magnificent," editor Atwood observed, and the might and power of nature inspired more than one muse.

In an essay published in the *Monitor* entitled "Wayside Reflections," a visitor who identified himself only as "DGP" wrote of standing on the bluff in language that, while antiquated in its phraseology, has been echoed in sentiment by more than one erosion watcher — and victim — in modern days:

"How fearful the monster has eaten into the soil, undermining the ground until even this spot upon which our feet rest becomes debatable ground. Awful thought! This summit of a bank must become food for the monster that shows its foam at our feet...Must we yield him inch by inch our ground which we take so much pride in? Must dwelling after dwelling be moved out of his reach as has been necessary heretofore? Oh, God in thy wisdom prevent the work of destruction! Stop it where it is!"

Author Joseph C. Lincoln, who owned a home on The Boulevard (now known as Shore Road) about a mile north of the lighthouses, wrote about visiting the scene in his book, *Cape Cod Yesterdays*. He was four years old at the time.

"They — the lights and brick houses — had stood on the high bluff at the southern end of Chatham village for years and our people had visited them often.

"But there was an especial reason for this particular visit. Old Ocean had been playing his tricks again. The storms of the two preceding winters had broken through the outer beach, the tides had widened the opening, and now, instead of standing safe and secure half a mile from the lines of surf, the twin lights were tottering precariously on the very edge of a rapidly caving 50 foot bank, with the curling breakers at its very foot. The government engineers had decided that they could not be protected or moved. A pair of new lighthouses and a new home for the keeper were in the process of erection a hundred yards back and on the other side of the road. The old ones were abandoned to tumble to destruction — which they eventually did.

"So, if our family were to see once more those old lighthouses intact, haste was essential. The visit was to be a sort of last look at the remains, so to speak."

The banks were indeed precarious; Hardy's daughter was watching the waves from the cliff one day in 1875 when the land beneath her feet suddenly gave way. She slid several feet downward but, luckily, stopped before reaching the waves "dashing furiously below," noted the *Monitor*. A rope was lowered and she was pulled to safety unhurt.

The south tower was 46 feet from the bluff's edge in January of 1878. An article in the January 8 *Monitor* made note of the continuing erosion, adding that "during the recent gales the beach has broken through in a new place, north of the station houses [located on South Beach]...endangering Stage Harbor."

As the breach expanded, the hopes for the new harbor faded. It had "so much filled between the beach and land near the [south] island" by March 1878, wrote Atwood, "that persons can pass across on foot, by a little wading, at low water." Indeed, Stage Harbor had become the town's new deep-water port. The prospect of the ocean's washing over the south beach and destroying the tenuous strip of land separating Stage Harbor from Chatham's inner harbor was seen as a threat to the fleet; tons of sand filling in Stage Harbor would be the likely result. It wasn't until 1886 that the bar between the mainland and Morris Island did break. It was not permanent, however, and the spit emerged and disappeared at various times over the next decades until a sand dike was built by the Army Corps of Engineers in 1958.

Expectations of the now-abandoned towers' imminent fall grew. Children hung around the spot, hoping to witness the inevitable. Boys waited for chunks of earth to fall from the bank and threw rocks at the snakes that emerged from their cool, dark hiding places. "Some people," noted the *Monitor*, "especially school boys, are already arranging to be there when the old buildings tumble over the banks."

It would be a long wait. On September 30, 1879, Hardy measured 27 inches between the south tower and the bank. Two months later, a third of the foundation hung in mid-air.

On Monday, December 15, Hardy reported fresh northwest gales and intermittent clouds. At twenty minutes to one in the afternoon, with about five people watching, the tower leaned over a bit, stopped, then cracked two or three feet above the foundation, pitchpoled over the bank and smashed to a thousand pieces below.

As people sat down to lunch, houses throughout the neighborhood trembled with the impact, the *Monitor* reported. "A multitude arrived," Atwood wrote, "much too late for the exhibition."

It was eight years and one month to the day from the 1871 breach.

By the next year, the erosion rate was slowing. The old keeper's house began its fall, bit by bit, in July; at the end of that month, however, Hardy wrote in his diary that "the Beach outside is Still making down very fast and is now nearly abreast of the lights. If it continues will Soon protect the shore." South Beach was breaking up faster and migrating toward the mainland, and North Beach's southerly march was already noticeable.

Finally, the north tower succumbed at 2 p.m. on March 26, 1881. By that summer, Hardy noticed that the westward stretching tip of South Beach was closing off the inner harbor. "Tide don't ran out while one year ago small vessels & fishing boats passed in and out of this channel," he wrote. Just four years before, the passage between the northern tip of South Beach and the mainland was nearly a half mile wide. On July 31, Hardy wrote that the opening had closed completely, which he hoped would offer "a safe protection to the station and shores." A month later, in Hardy's final North Beach-related diary entry, he wrote that "the Beach is growing stronger verry fast."

Tally of one decade's losses to erosion: two lighthouses, one keeper's house, at least a dozen (and probably more) homes forced to relocate, an access road serving a half dozen houses wiped out, and several hundred feet chopped off the ends of Holway and Water streets.

South Beach continued to break up over the next few decades. Various configurations resulted; at one point, low-lying marshes and sand flats built up from the mainland below the lights. Stretched thin, the remnants of South Beach at one point connected to the northern tip of Monomoy, forming one continuous island. The beach beneath James' Bluff grew wide for a time, much as it did in the late 1990s, but this eventually eroded away as well, exposing the high bluff to the ocean once again.

Concerned over the possibility of continuing erosion, property owners atop the bluff from Water Street to the lighthouses barged in tons of granite boulders from Quincy and packed them tightly against the foot of the bank. Giese cites an article in the January 31, 1933 *Boston Globe* stating the town "rip-rapped" the banking to further protect the lighthouses.

J. Clinton Hammond was a young man then, and until his dying day he believed those rocks saved the land and buildings he called home, three houses north of the lighthouse. When erosion began in earnest in the late 1980s, he advocated the same solution; but it was easier for property owners, and the town, for that matter, to take things into their own hands a generation earlier, when the idea of environmental protection of shorefront land was radical and unheard of.

Whether or not those boulders were necessary is arguable. But they appear to have done their job, as there was little appreciable erosion of the mainland as North Beach continued to build southward. Those old rocks would also become important later on, providing an excuse for federal and state officials to bend the rules slightly and expedite the augmentation and modernization of the original revetment.

By the early 20th century, Chatham had become a more resort-oriented community. On North Beach, hunting camps had been established in the 1870s, simple, rustic shacks for the most part, shelter for the hunters who took advantage of the wild fowl and exotic migratory shorebirds that preferred the isolated beach. They joined the Old Harbor Lifesaving Station, a fixture on the beach since the middle of the 19th century (eventually floated to Provincetown where today it has been restored by the Cape Cod National Seashore). The shacks were tenuous things; Joe Nickerson recalls his father's camp, acquired when half of another old shack washed away in 1928. The beach washed over in the same spot 10 years later, taking out the remainder of the camp, but ironically leaving the hunting camp's most treasured asset, its stove, still standing stark and alone in a sea of sand.

Chatham experienced a steep drop in population in the early years of the twentieth century. The population went from 2,411 in 1870, when 71 percent of the inhabitants worked in the maritime and fisheries-related industries, to 1,667 in 1915, a 31 percent loss, due, apparently, to a depression in the fisheries and a decline in shipping. But the modern age, and a concurrent shift in the economic base, was coming to Chatham. In 1887, the Old Colony Railroad, a branch of the New Haven Railroad, opened a spur running from Harwich center into the heart of Chatham. Tourism and the summer resort business boomed. Large, fancy hotels like the Mattaquason Inn, the Chatham Hotel, the Rose Acres Inn, the Old Harbor Inn and the Chatham Bars Inn (the only one still remaining) opened. Fishing still remained the biggest year-round employer through the 1940s, but the writing was in the sand. New highways and the post-World War II boom fueled an insatiable appetite for recreation and tourism which engulfed the Cape in general.

By then the beach had migrated almost as far south as the single lighthouse; the old north tower was moved to Eastham in 1923 (its base is still visible on the north side of the front lawn of the Coast Guard Station). More camps had sprung up on the beach, many constructed haphazardly of scrap wood and driftwood, but all with personality and, of course, distinctive outhouses. By now the cottages were used as vacation getaways as much as hunting camps.

Through the 1950s and 1960s, the most dramatic changes occurred not to North Beach but to Monomoy and Morris Islands. At one point, both connected to the mainland. Victor Goldsmith notes that the thin strip of sand between Morris Island and the mainland frequently washed away only to build up again. In 1958, the cut between Morris Island and the mainland was open, and sand choked Stage Harbor. A coalition of property owners and town officials eager to promote development of the island secured more than $400,000 in local, state and federal money to have the harbor dredged and the spoil used to build a sand dike between Little Beach and Morris Island. There was so much sand that marshes were filled and later built on.

Monomoy remained connected to Morris Island just south of the current location of the U.S. Fish and Wildlife's Monomoy Wildlife Refuge headquarters until the early 1960s, when a channel appeared, apparently mysteriously. There is still controversy over whether this was a man-made canal or the result of natural causes. Whichever was responsible, that particular cut widened in subsequent storms until Monomoy became the island it is today (the great storm of February 1978 further divided Monomoy into two islands, the smaller, barren North Island and the larger South Island, home to numerous endangered shorebirds and the old lighthouse, which was listed on the National Registry of Historic Places in the 1970s).

In August 1961, President John F. Kennedy signed a law establishing the Cape Cod National Seashore, 39 miles of shorefront land, more than 43,000 acres, stretching from the Province Lands at the Cape's end to the southern tip of North Beach. Monomoy was excluded because it was already protected as a National Wildlife Refuge, a status first discussed in the late 1920s but not bestowed until 1944, after it was used as a practice bombing range during World War II.

Morris Island was also left out of the Cape Cod National Seashore — although initially slated for inclusion — for several purported reasons, including the access it provided to Monomoy and a fear that public beach facilities would attract too many people (at one time state officials talked about a 2,000-car parking lot with bathhouse facilities on Morris and Monomoy islands). In the end, however, it was political machinations by Chatham officials and people with a vested interest in the fate of Morris and Stage islands which successfully snipped the southern terminus of the Great Beach from the national seashore plans.

Shortly before the Cape Cod National Seashore came into being, a lawsuit filed over ownership of North Beach was resolved and the beach was parceled out to the original heirs of those given ownership more than a century earlier. But the beach was included within the boundaries of the new national seashore, and when the U.S. Park Service took over in 1962, those who had owned camps on North Beach that were built before September 1, 1959, were allowed to retain ownership. Still other parcels, developed after that date, the government took by eminent domain but granted the owners tenancy that expired in the late 1990s; many have since renegotiated lease arrangements and continue to occupy their camps. A lot of unimproved land was acquired by the government, but much of the beach had already been acquired by the town of Chatham, through various gifts and purchases made over the years. Strict zoning regulations, requiring six-acre lots, reduced the possibility of future development on the beach to zero.

In the mid 1960s, recreational use of North Beach escalated significantly. The discovery of Cape Cod as the state's premier summer recreation resort area spread to still-rural towns like Chatham and Orleans. The advent of affordable four-wheel drive trucks and jeeps made the beach even more attractive and accessible, eventually forcing the towns of Chatham and Orleans into regulating vehicle use of the barrier beach. The only way onto the beach, except by boat, was through the Nauset Beach parking area in East Orleans; there a gate shack was set up and beach-use stickers sold to control access by the general public. Orleans handled the administrative side, and Chatham assumed the job of law enforcement patrols of the eight-mile long sand spit, an arrangement that still holds today.

By the early 1960s, conditions in the harbor were deteriorating rapidly. The inlet, now south of Morris Island, was badly shoaled and considered cautious ground for even the most experienced captain. Fearing the impact of an uncontrolled breach, Chatham's selectmen asked Congressman Hastings Keith to file legislation for a comprehensive Army Corps of Engineers study of the Nauset/Pleasant Bay/Monomoy system. "Commercial fisheries benefits," read a letter from the selectmen, "would be greatly enhanced."

The study began in 1964 with a meeting at Chatham High School to solicit public input. The official stance of the town, as expressed in a statement issued to the Army Corps, was that the continued growth of North Beach was making passage out of the harbor "precarious and erratic," and that the hazardous channel "endangers the lives of those using it and decreases the number of trips to fishing grounds."

Town officials were also worried about development along the shoreline, which had exploded, the previous bout with erosion apparently forgotten. "A natural, uncontrolled break through Nauset could cause inestimable damage to shore-front properties and, if resulting in a semi-landlocked condition, could be disastrous to the fishing industry."

Finally in 1967, the corps issued a proposal. After three years of study, their findings were certainly no surprise to the locals. The Corps report stated that "...navigation facilities in Pleasant Bay are inadequate for the commercial fishery and recreational fleets, both existing and prospective." In continued, "if no navigational improvements are made in the area, it is expected that the existing Chatham Harbor inlet will, in the not too distant future, close completely."

The Pleasant Bay Project, as it was known, was both bold and controversial. The corps proposed building an artificial inlet, 1,000 wide, through the beach opposite Chatham Light. It would be supported by two rock jetties, each 1,600 feet long, the northern jetty designed to trap southern drifting sand which would be periodically pumped across the inlet to nourish the downdrift beach. A navigable channel, 200 feet wide and 20 feet deep at low water, would be maintained through the inlet.

It didn't stop there. The corps proposed closing the existing inlet between North Beach and Monomoy with a sand dike composed of spoil dredged from between Monomoy and Morris Island, where a channel from Nantucket Sound into Chatham Harbor would be created.

When the selectmen first contacted Congressman Keith, the cost of a project of this type was thought to be between $4 to $8 million. By 1968, the corps was using a figure of $14,900,000, 69 percent paid by the federal government, which would also pick up the $544,000 tab for annual jetty maintenance and dredging. Massachusetts, Chatham, Orleans and Harwich would divvy up the remaining costs, since all would ostensibly benefit.

The idea of duplicating nature — really hastening the inevitable — had its proponents. Congress authorized it, but in an overtly political move, provided no funding. Governor Francis Sargent, who had a home on Pleasant Bay in East Orleans, endorsed the plan. Wharfinger Harold Claflin put together some interesting figures intended to show the benefit to the fishing industry: Between 1945 and 1967, nine lives were lost going over the Chatham Bars; there were five near-fatalities,

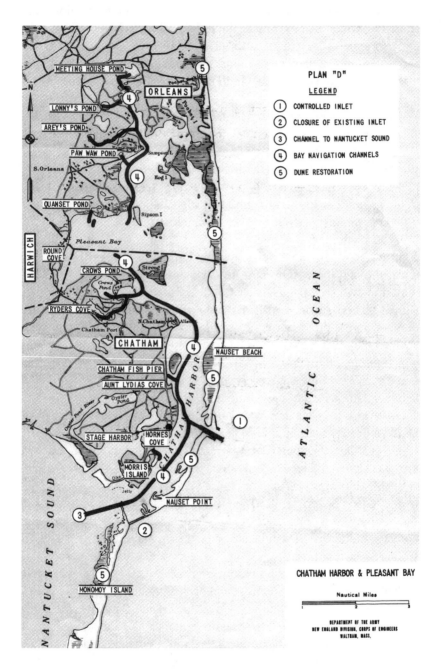

PLAN "D"

LEGEND

① CONTROLLED INLET
② CLOSURE OF EXISTING INLET
③ CHANNEL TO NANTUCKET SOUND
④ BAY NAVIGATION CHANNELS
⑤ DUNE RESTORATION

CHATHAM HARBOR & PLEASANT BAY

Nautical Miles

DEPARTMENT OF THE ARMY
NEW ENGLAND DIVISION, CORPS OF ENGINEERS
WALTHAM, MASS.

THE FINAL PLANS FOR THE U. S. ARMY CORPS OF ENGINEER'S PLEASANT BAY PROJECT.

four boats sank and more than $12,500 in annual damage to fishing vessels — windscreens blown out, pilot houses crushed, hulls bent and punctured. Richard Larsen, then manager of the Chatham Fishermen's Cooperative, was quoted in a newspaper article as saying the vastly safer conditions created by a stable inlet would encourage fishermen to venture offshore an additional 50 days a year.

Few fishermen were enthusiastic about the plan, however, and many were downright skeptical that it would work. And it was the fishermen's backing the proposal needed; the corps held the group's interest as its top priority. One of the main criteria in deciding to undertake the project was that the economic benefit to the fishing industry and its trickle down effect in town had to be greater than or equal to the costs that would be incurred. Some fishermen worried that opening the harbor up would attract larger vessels, increase competition and edge out the small commercial fishermen, who made up the majority of the fleet. Shellfishermen wondered what would happen to the productive shellfish beds in Pleasant Bay and the Common Flats around Monomoy. Any economic benefit, many felt, would also have its drawbacks.

Most residents weren't very happy with the idea, either.

"What they're doing, is, they're playing on the beaches of the Lord, and I hope they know what they are doing," the *Boston Globe* quoted one local man.

More delays, more costs. By 1971, it was up to $18 million.

The Massachusetts Water Resource Commission and other environmental groups rejected the plan, for the most part because it didn't have the support of local fishermen. Sensing the waning interest and mounting opposition, the selectmen let the project ebb.

The Pleasant Bay Project "died on the vine," in the words of David Ryder, a selectman at the time, who also happened to be a commercial fisherman. Had it gone through, Chatham's shoreline would undoubtedly be very different. Yet there is considerable doubt whether it would have worked; the corps' plans were based on observations and paperwork. The government planned to spend a quarter of a million dollars on a physical model to study the artificial channel's effects on tidal flow and water temperature — the results of which may have sunk the project — but it was never built. Officially, the money wasn't there. Perhaps, however, the corps realized that the model might not have proved out and that the entire project had little chance of taming the natural geological forces that had shaped the beach for centuries.

THE STORY OF CHATHAM'S NORTH BEACH   **43**

So the barrier beach process continued undisturbed. The beach became narrower as it overlapped the northern edge of Monomoy and washovers become more frequent. The great storm of February 1978, which dumped several feet of snow on most of the state, claimed scores of homes along the South Shore and split Monomoy in two. It worked over North Beach as well, picking up and moving camps hundreds of feet in massive washovers. No permanent breach occurred, though. Wary townspeople kept a keen eye out.

The tidal exchange between Pleasant Bay and the ocean became more restricted as the beach grew south. The harbor and bay were placid, their waters warm, encouraging even greater recreational use. Only three feet of water flowed over the outside bar at low tide, and the difference in tidal levels between the inner harbor and the Atlantic widened. Flows were so sluggish that before there could be a full exchange of waters from low to high tide between the harbor and the ocean, the tide changed. Water quality took a nose dive, especially in the upper reaches of Pleasant Bay. Environmentalists began to worry that the estuary, one of the largest and most productive in the state, would be destroyed. Eutrophication, the slow choking of life from a body of water by stagnation, began to set in.

By the mid 1980s, North Beach was a low, flat, sandy stretch of land less than a mile across the harbor. Four-wheel drive vehicles darted up and down its length, for the most part sticking to established trails or the hardened sand of the outer beach. But the stretch of beach that had protected the harbor, and the lighthouse, for a generation was growing increasingly barren. Environmentalists debated the benefits of putting up snow fences, pallets or used Christmas trees to catch sand — yet it was done anyway, sometimes by town groups, sometimes by individual camp owners, sometimes anonymously.

The particular section of beach across from the Coast Guard station had been low and narrow for years. The east/west vehicle trails were closed down in an attempt to prevent it from shrinking even more. If a break was to come, it would come here, there was little doubt. All the snow fencing in the world couldn't stop it.

Then, on a very cold, wet January afternoon on the second day of a new year, a handful of people watching from the lighthouse overlook saw what is often discussed but seldom seen: history repeating itself.

BREAKTHROUGH

L ate in December 1986, a few early winter storms sent huge white-
caps hurtling against North Beach's outer shore. Observers at
the Chatham Lighthouse overlook could clearly see the roiling,
spewing breakers foaming above the low dune line like white icing on
a sandy cake. There were occasional washovers which flattened veg-
etation and swept away dunes, but they were temporary. When the sky
cleared and seas calmed, the beach remained more or less unscathed.

Later, the winter turned into the worst of the decade, perhaps in
half a century. More than 40 inches of snow fell, and the Cape, especially the outer Cape, shut down completely for days at a time. Most
of the effects were, however, temporary; snow melted and power came
back on. But one particular storm, mild in contrast to what came later,
will nonetheless go down in history as the progenitor of an event which
would be felt for years to come.

There was snow early on the day of Friday, January 2, 1987. The
air had turned bitter and winds whipped around from the northeast.
All week the tides had been extremely high due to a celestial phenomenon called syzygy, an alignment of the Earth, sun and moon that oc-
curs every nine years. This year there was an added factor, a concurrent alignment of several planets, which happens only once in every 35
years.

Syzygy, along with a full moon tide, accounted for perhaps two to
three feet in extra tidal height that day. By early morning, a full-fledged
northeaster, packing sustained winds of 50 miles per hour (with gusts
of 68 miles per hour recorded at the National Weather Service station
on Morris Island), added a storm surge of eight to 12 feet.

Breakers 10 to 12 feet high crashed over the narrow strip of North

Beach opposite the lighthouse. High tide arrived at 1 p.m., and a crowd gathered at the overlook to watch as the Atlantic surged across the approximately 100-yard-wide beach and flowed into Chatham Harbor. Several other portions of the beach were similarly inundated by the January 2 storm. But at low tide the following day everyone in Chatham saw, for the first time in decades, a permanent channel linking the inner harbor with the Atlantic, isolating a three-and-a-half mile section of the beach.

I traveled down the beach early Saturday morning, at dawn, with Lieutenant Wayne Love of the Chatham police department. As we rode along the outer beach in the department's four-wheel drive pickup, he pointed out the various washovers and what had been high, solid-looking dunes torn apart by the storm. Arriving opposite the lighthouse, which still threw its warning beacon seaward against the cloud-shrouded early morning sky, we found a meandering stream in the center of a vast, football field-sized washout. Approximately 18 feet wide, a foot or so deep, the channel seemed natural, nonthreatening, even beautiful in its undulating simplicity. Water flowed through at a good clip, but it would not have been unthinkable for someone in waders or even a good pair of boots to ford across.

Love had for years overseen the law enforcement aspect of the beach, which included keeping the various trails maintained so beach buggies and other off-road vehicles could travel the length of the beach. It was a popular place, not only with those who owned camps here, but also for weekenders, many of whom came nearly every weekend of the year and were just as much a part of the beach as the beach grass and shallow ponds. Over the years, Love saw the beach move around a lot, and he knew something significant had happened. The magnitude of the story didn't hit me for a week or so, when I began educating myself about the barrier beach and listening to people like Love, who had seen geology happen right in front of their eyes.

Immediately there was speculation that the gap would close up with the next tide. Yet water continued to flow at both high and low tide, scouring the channel more at each exchange. Several days after the breakthrough occurred, Harbormaster Peter Ford took an aerial view of the beach and said a mushroom-shaped plume of sand extended 150 yards into the harbor from the cut, and a bar was building up on the outside, classic signs of a nascent inlet.

Recognizing that the new cut could be the one predicted by Dr.

A BREAK IS BORN: LOOKING BACK TOWARD TOWN FROM NORTH BEACH THE MORNING AFTER THE STORM THAT CREATED THE BREAKTHROUGH.

ONE YEAR LATER.

THE STORY OF CHATHAM'S NORTH BEACH   47

Graham Giese in his 1978 report, and realizing the potential impact, the selectmen held a hastily called meeting the Monday after the storm to discuss possible remedial measures.

Ford told me after the meeting that "the consensus of the town fathers is to let nature take its course. There will be no preventive measures." This hands-off policy was to later become a key issue in the controversy surrounding the shoreline erosion that began in earnest ten months later. But Ford summed up most people's attitude in the days immediately following the initial breakthrough when he said, when asked about the possibility of the cut closing: "I wouldn't put five cents on it either way."

Within two weeks it was clear that the cut was rapidly establishing itself as an inlet and wasn't going to close up immediately, as some thought. Scouring had produced a 500-foot-wide channel with respectable depths at both low and high tides, enough to allow the 42-foot fishing vessel *Asylum* to pass through at half tide. Almost overnight fishermen switched from the 45-minute trip to the Atlantic via the old Chatham Bars inlet, between North Beach and Monomoy, to the more direct and time-saving cut-through, just a few minutes' steaming time from the fish pier at Aunt Lydia's Cove.

The shortcut wasn't without hazards; the current ran six to seven knots and the channel itself was treacherous and could change configuration in the time it took to complete a day's fishing. Fishermen, however, aren't known for their trepidation, and most decided the time saved was worth the risk. The fact that there were no serious injuries or accidents in those early days, when the breach was still in its early stages of formation, says something about the navigational skills of Chatham's fishermen, and the extreme care and caution practiced by local boaters.

As soon as he was informed of the situation, Dr. Giese visited the scene and started taking measurements and photographs. In late January, Dr. Giese and Dr. David Aubrey, also of the Woods Hole Oceanographic Institute, proposed a study of the breakthrough's effect on tidal ranges, salinity levels and the distribution of sediment throughout the system. The idea was to observe the much-described barrier beach process in action, and develop a computer model that would allow scientists to accurately predict when breaks would occur in other barrier beaches.

Giese installed computerized gauges to measure changes in tide level at the fish pier, at Meetinghouse Pond in Orleans — the head of Pleasant Bay — as well as offshore instruments to measure wave and current strength. Eventually funded by Chatham to the tune of $26,000, the study used aerial photographs, shoreline profiles from six locations from the Cow Yard Landing to Morris Island, and transit measurements at the ends of North and South Beach taken from the lighthouse. The results would be useful to the town in the future in developing a management plan for the Chatham Harbor waters and shoreline, Dr. Giese said.

Through January and February, the area was battered by two more northeast storms, with huge snowfalls and winds up to 80 miles per hour. At first the breach widened by as much as 1,000 feet in two weeks; but as it became more established and organized, the rate of growth slowed to perhaps 100 or so feet per week, as a mean average. In early March the breach was 1,710 feet wide, with a main channel 20 feet deep. Dr. Giese, at the time, was guarded in his predictions about the fate of the cut-through, but left little doubt about where his attention was focused. "We can't say at this moment for certain that this particular break is the one that will stay open," he said. "But we can say that the characteristics associated with this break indicate the conditions are right."

Most of the initial interest in the breach came from scientists, local historians and environmentalists, fishermen, and the people who owned or rented camps on North Beach. The impact on the latter group was minimal; there were no camps south of the breach, almost all of it town-owned, and that fragile section of the spit had been off-limits to vehicles for some time. Mainland dwellers, the people in the million-dollar houses along Shore Road and side roads that trail toward the shore like fishing lines, seemed curious, but were silent. That didn't last long.

It didn't take long for the break to make its presence known along Chatham's eastern shoreline. In early February, high tides swamped the foot of the parking lot at the end of Andrew Harding's Lane and poured over the fish pier bulkhead a mile north. The harbor tide levels, thanks to a more efficient tidal exchange between the harbor and Pleasant Bay and the ocean, increased water levels throughout the system by as much as one foot. Tides were consequently also nearly a foot lower, exposing bars and sand flats that had lain submerged for decades. It became possible to walk, at low tide, from the Cow Yard

Landing to Tern Island without getting your feet wet.

But the most important and far-reaching effect of the break was only beginning to manifest itself. By early February, Charles Horne noticed that the beach in front of his property, south of the lighthouse, was disappearing. It soon became clear that the tidal changes wrought by the break were conspiring to erode away sand in front of more than 20 properties in the area south of Lighthouse Beach known as Little Beach, between the Chatham Beach and Tennis Club and Outermost Harbor. Horne applied for emergency permission to put sand on the beach, a process referred to as nourishing the beach; the Conservation Commission turned him down because the situation didn't qualify as an emergency, defined under the Massachusetts Wetland Protection Act as an imminent threat to the "health and safety" of the public.

By early March as much as 20 feet of beach and dune was gone from Little Beach, much of it apparently washed into the basin of Outermost Harbor Marine, a small marina located in the nook between Little Beach and the marshes that presage Morris Island. Sand filled in around the bulkheads that were six feet deep before the break, and many boats were aground inside the basin at low tide. Owners Thomas and Linda Marshall applied for and received town and state permission to dredge 1,500 cubic feet of sand, which eventually turned into a regular program of maintenance dredging in the basin and channel, a classic struggle against the forces of nature. By summer, the Marshalls were wondering how long their business could support the expensive maintenance (they eventually purchased a dredge, and later sold the marina).

Officials were in a quandary over how to deal with the problems that were cropping up with alarming frequency. What type of erosion control measures were permissible? What *should* be allowed? Where did the town's jurisdiction end and that of the state and federal governments begin? With an association of Little Beach property owners poised to file a request for permission to take steps to save their rapidly eroding property, on March 24, state, federal and local officials held their first meeting to thrash out a policy for addressing the anticipated problems. It was to be the first of many. In years to come, state environmental officials were to become very familiar with Chatham.

Attended by representatives of the town's Conservation Commission, Board of Selectmen, the Massachusetts Department of Environmental Quality Engineering (later changed to the Department of Envi-

BREAKTHROUGH

ronmental Protection [DEP]), the office of Coastal Zone Management (CZM), the Army Corps of Engineers, National Park Service, Congressman Gerry E Studds' office and state representative Howard Cahoon, Jr., the meeting centered on the what, where and how of erosion control measures. Taking their cue from the state wetlands act, regulatory honchos told local ConCom members that so-called "hard solutions" — engineered structures such as revetments and seawalls — were prohibited, at least in the Little Beach area. Beach nourishment, planting of dune grass, and, at most, sand-filled environmentally-safe bags were the only "soft" alternative the commission was expected to approve. Time frame for permitting was another major topic. Obtaining the necessary permissions from state and federal regulators for any "hard" erosion control or for work below the waterline, apart from emergency measures, would take six months to a year.

Property owners weren't particularly happy with this, nor were they encouraged by the fact that the session failed to produce a cohesive defense plan against shoreline erosion. The Little Beach Waterfront Property Owners Group nonetheless moved forward with their petition to nourish their beach. By April, the tide had eaten away another 10 to 15 feet, and high water lapped at the doorsteps of at least one cottage. Prevailing northeast winds skewed the waves coming through the break in their direction, organizer William Doggett, Jr. said, cutting across the beach like a hot knife through butter.

Conservation Commission approval came swiftly, and sand dredged from Outermost Harbor Marine was trucked a few hundred feet up the road and deposited on Little Beach. Later, Doggett and his neighbors applied for and received the go-ahead to armor their rapidly disappearing dunes with hundreds of small sandbags that appeared to do the job. The erosion subsided by summer, and by fall a substantial expanse of beach had accreted.

South Beach, as tradition dictated the amputated section of North Beach be called, was also becoming a subject of concern. The U.S. Fish and Wildlife Service let the town know they were very interested in the island due to its increasing attractiveness as a nesting area for piping plovers and least terns, two protected shorebird species. In previous years the birds had nested on the end of North Beach, but the new island's isolation as well as the regular washovers — providing a perfect habitat for the plovers — promised less intrusion by man, the agency claimed, and would provide an ideal nesting alternative to

Monomoy Island, where seagulls had displaced the smaller birds. Although several pairs of birds (of both species) did establish nests on the island that first summer, most were either destroyed by washovers or fell victim to the few foxes and skunks trapped on the island, despite attempts at management by the Massachusetts Audubon Society. It was to be several years before significant numbers of the birds began to nest on the island.

The whole question of use and management of South Beach was under debate by April. Police Chief Barry Eldredge predicted it would be the most popular beach on the Cape because of its isolation. That engendered concern for safety, since the only way to reach the island was by boat, and the most convenient landing area was right where the currents swirled and the surf tousled angrily. Officially under the aegis of the Park Commission — that section of the barrier beach was given to the town by Joshua Nickerson earlier in the decade — South Beach had already been the scene of one incident, when some local residents ferried several three-wheeled, over-sand vehicles across the harbor and proceeded to run rampant over the entire island. Eventually, a "hands-off" approach was adopted, establishing itself as the dominant government policy regarding the breach. There would be no patrols during the summer, foot or otherwise, and any emergencies would be dealt with as they came up. Later, after washovers and shoaling created a land bridge between South Beach and Lighthouse Beach — only at low tide, at first — there were other worries. Someone would undoubtedly become stranded, since the window of opportunity for pedestrian passage was less than an hour. In the winter of 1988, someone did in fact make the trek on foot across the harbor, with the assistance of naught but a pair of waders. (The Naturist Society, a nudist group, also put out the word that South Beach's isolation made it perfect for nude sunbathing. Chatham selectmen, as always, took this in stride, but the Park Commission quickly adopted an ordinance banning nudity on all public beaches, complete with a very explicit description of what constituted nudity.)

The break, by then three-quarters of a mile wide, raised other questions of public safety, for boaters and swimmers alike. The Coast Guard's 44-foot rescue vessel docked at the fish pier was aground at low tide and could navigate in the harbor only about eight hours a day. Great surf conditions attracted windsurfers, and one was drawn out toward the open sea through the cut in February and barely managed to struggle back to shore. Water in the harbor was much colder. Ocean-sized waves sometimes broke on the inner shore and driftwood and other flotsam and jetsam were turning up, some the result of erosion. Small boats could no longer anchor in parts of the harbor.

In mid-April the town issued, through the Coast Guard, a notice to mariners warning of the "very hazardous" conditions in the new inlet. The inlet, said Harbormaster Peter Ford, was deceptive; on an incoming tide it might be as placid as an inland pond. But when the tide turned, the surf kicked up and the currents became tricky and dangerous. It was even worse with the slightest off-shore breeze. The worry was not for fishermen, virtually all of them experienced sailors who nonetheless had trouble navigating the cut, but recreational boaters unfamiliar with local waters. Ford was unwilling to mark the channel with buoys; he had neither the capacity nor the equipment to sink markers strong enough to withstand the cut's intense currents.

Signs were posted at 16 town landings around Pleasant Bay and Chatham Harbor warning of the changing conditions. Twenty thousand flyers, with the strangely endearing title "Some Things You Should Know About the New Chatham Harbor Inlet," were distributed to hotels, marinas, boatyards and other public places. "Currents in the inlet are ferocious," the bright orange broadside read, "and can sweep an

THE TOWN PARKING LOT AT ANDREW HARDING'S LANE RAVAGED BY THE OCEAN IN LATE 1987.

unsuspecting swimmer, a small boat, sailboat or sailboard out to the cold ocean or into dangerous surf."

On North Beach itself, erosion continued to eat away at both inner and outer shorelines, and the high tides brought water levels dangerously close to some camps that faced the harbor. Several vehicle trails were wiped out, but no camps were in immediate danger. In the late spring, Chatham and Orleans officials decided to cut in half the daily limit of vehicles allowed on the beach, since the three southernmost miles of beach were no longer accessible. The focus of erosion began to shift as spring weather patterns kicked in.

On April 3, a milestone of sorts occurred with the first break-related legal action. Maurice Hartley, owner of a waterfront house off Wilkey Way, a quarter mile south of Claflin Landing and a few hundred yards north of Holway Street, obtained an injunction against the Conservation Commission which prohibited the group from interfering in efforts to halt erosion of his beach.

"When you're standing there and the place is washing away at six feet per week, you don't have time to go through the whole process," Hartley said in a telephone interview from his Virginia Beach home. "The court order is to shortcut the whole procedure." Hartley's complaint said 40 feet of beach had been lost since the breach and continued to disappear at a rate of one foot per day. His attorney had attended the March 24 meeting, out of which he expected an emergency management plan to emerge; nothing materialized, and that non-action was one of the bases of Hartley's suit. The move came as a complete surprise to Chatham officials. Hartley had never even informed the ConCom of the need or desire to protect his property.

Hartley installed a few concrete bags along the foot of his dune, but the injunction only tied the hands of the town; it failed to name state or federal government agencies, an oversight that prevented the owner from taking more extensive measures, such as revetment or bulkhead construction, which had to follow the lengthy permitting process he was hoping to avoid.

Giese, meanwhile, told 200 people attending a forum on the breach that as much as 47 feet of dune had eroded between Holway Street and Little Beach since the January 2 cut opened. A one-mile stretch of shoreline was under heaviest bombardment; both to the north and south erosion was slight and, in fact, some accretion was taking place. The shoreline, said the scientist, was undergoing a process of "straightening."

Late spring arrived and the situation seemed to calm down, although the overlook area was constantly crowded. There was a marked increase in business that summer, and a few people even designed "Breakthrough" T-shirts and sold them in local shops. A Boston television station aired a long profile of Chatham and the break in late May, piquing the curiosity of even more people.

Unsolicited advice on how to handle the situation poured into the selectmen's office, thanks to the extensive coverage of the breach by the *New York Times* and other far-flung newspapers, along with a full-page spread in *Time*. One letter suggested that the town take a cue from the Dutch and build a dike; another said the only way to close the breach was to sink a freighter across the opening. Perhaps, ventured another, thousands of old tires could be anchored inside the harbor opposite the cut to serve as a breakwater against incoming waves. Town officials, in the midst of a reorganization of Chatham's government, found most of the advice impractical, if not downright bizarre.

In early June, Giese toured Outermost Harbor Marine and several town landings, lingering at Andrew Harding's Lane, where ocean-sized waves crashed on a shore that had formerly been a peaceful and placid bathing beach favored by families with children. The once expansive and sandy beach was mostly under water at high tide, had dropped vertically from its level earlier in the year and a large berm of sand had built up at the foot of the parking lot. On extreme high tides, even that didn't stop the tide from lapping onto the asphalt. Behind the parking lot and between Andrew Harding's Lane and Holway Street was an even lower wetlands area, not to mention half a dozen homes.

Giese recommended in a report to the Conservation Commission that about 50 feet of the parking area be removed and an artificial dune built across it, connecting dunes to the north and south. Of the seven town landings immediately fronting the harbor, Andrew Harding's Lane was "the most severely out of adjustment with shore conditions," Giese wrote. The commission endorsed the recommendation and passed it along to the selectmen, who control town landings.

While they noted the suggestion, the town fathers chose, again, to do nothing. Police Chief Eldredge objected to the loss of the parking area, and argued that the asphalt would be better protection against the ocean's onslaught than a sand dune. Selectmen, looking into empty and echoing town coffers, finally judged the proposal unworkable. There were also concerns over assuring public access to an extremely popular beach, and a complacent attitude prevailed as erosion abated somewhat in the summer. Besides, they were busy with other things, including trying to get John McGrath to stop using the Andrew Harding's Landing as a departure and pickup point for his North Beach ferry service (which nature succeeded in doing eventually).

Money was allocated by the state for a second study of the system in July. Giese planned to use the $80,000 to develop bathymetric and offshore data, as opposed to the onshore study being funded by the town. August brought word of yet another study, as Congressman Studds announced that the Army Corps of Engineers planned a $300,000 reconnaissance study of the stability of the inlet, mainland erosion, the effects of drifting sand and the impact on commercial fishing and recreational boating. It was the second corps study of the Nauset Barrier Beach system in less than 50 years. Like its predecessor, it too would have a long life, but a somewhat more affirmative conclusion.

After viewing the area from a helicopter with fellow Representative Henry Nowak, chairman of the House Subcommittee on Water Resources, Studds said the corps had done a massive amount of preparatory work in proposing the study and was particularly interested in the North Beach break because it represented a barrier beach in a completely natural state — unencumbered by man-made structures like jetties, groins and major buildings. Like Giese's study, the Army corps plan was aimed at developing a model applicable to other barrier beaches.

"Obviously the immediate concern is at the local level," commented Studds, who was to be instrumental in steering the study and later ones, sometimes rescuing federal involvement from bureaucratic waters even rougher than the break. Congress eventually approved the study, and half the money was allocated for the first phase, which began in June 1988. Expected to take a year, the reconnaissance study would, according to project manager Susan Scott, determine whether the benefits of a federal harbor project for Chatham would justify expenditure of what would undoubtedly be millions of tax dollars.

As the summer wore on, the breach grew steadily wider. The expected emergencies failed to materialize, much to the relief of the police and fire departments, as well as the Coast Guard. There was little erosion of consequence; most of the area along the harbor actually gained beach during the calm season. Then, like an avenging marauder, September arrived.

Four days of high course tides sent waves rolling over half the parking lot at Andrew Harding's Lane and chewed up pavement at the end of Holway Street. More than a half mile wide now, after holding back all summer, the breach opened wide and let the ocean charge through and have at the unprotected shoreline between the two streets. Over a single weekend, almost 30 feet of beach was eliminated. Snow fences erected by some property owners over the summer failed to capture new sand, and were in turn swept away. By late September, at least 50 feet of low-lying beach and dune was gone, leaving some homes with less than 30 feet between the high water mark and their doorstep, where once there had been 200 feet of smooth, expansive beach and dune. Police barricaded the end of Holway Street after waves surrounded and isolated a catch basin, cutting the pavement off and creating a four-foot drop to the beach.

Frederick Rolfe, who owned the cottage adjacent to the Andrew Harding's Lane parking lot, placed sandbags around the perimeter of his property to keep flood waters from reaching the structure. "I don't know what to do," Rolfe said on September 21. "If we have a full moon tide and a northeaster this winter, that's all she wrote."

He couldn't have known how closely nature had been listening.

By the end of the month, Rolfe's attorney was threatening to sue the town if steps weren't taken to protect the parking lot, which was at least partially covered by water on a normal high tide. The edge of the asphalt was completely covered by drifting sand which was swept away and built up on alternative tides. The attorney, John Devereaux of Boston, argued that the creation of the parking lot in the 1950s, and the inaction of officials since the breach, left the town open to liability should substantial damage occur.

Bruce Gilmore, Chatham's town attorney, didn't see things that way. He told the selectmen that if "the town does nothing and nature takes its course and hurts those buildings, it's hard luck for those people." But if some sort of remedial action were to be taken and damage resulted anyway, then "we own those buildings."

When officials gathered at the parking lot at the end of September, its appearance had changed dramatically from the beginning of the summer. The high berm of sand had been obliterated. An old, decaying wooden bulkhead, which no one could remember ever seeing before, poked its rotted upper reaches out of the surf at low tide. A small shack once used as a halfway house by the old Lifesaving Service, the precursor to the Coast Guard — one of only two left in New England, it was listed on the National Register of Historic Places — was rescued from the charging sea and dragged back from the receding dune line just south of the parking lot.

The erosion season had begun, and before it was over, it would cause more damage to property and emotions than anything seen in Chatham in more than a century.

THIS VIEW OF THE CHANNEL INTO THE FISH PIER CLEARLY SHOWS THE EXTENSIVE SHOAL-ING THE BREAK CAUSED.

BREAKTHROUGH

BREACH

Fall came on strong, digging its claws into the fruits of the mild summer and flailing madly. By the standards of Cape Cod, there were no major storms, but the wind howled off the violently churning harbor, driving the frantic waves farther and farther inland. Even when the sun shone high and only a cool breeze tempered the warm air, waves still rushed through the gaping breach and smashed against fragile dunes. Ahead were the annual moon tides of the fall — nine, ten, eleven feet above normal — and the promise of a Chatham winter, even at its mildest a deadly enemy of the shoreline.

Those thoughts undoubtedly coursed through the minds of 10 people who met for the first time on Saturday morning, October 3. Their property was being stolen from beneath their very noses even as they sat in John Whelan's living room, a large picture window providing a panoramic view of the collective foe, the breach. All summer long the ocean had been kind to them, giving up hundreds of thousands of cubic yards of sand, making their soft, rolling beaches larger than ever. Now the time had come to ante up, and the sea, intent on collecting, sent in its strike force to reclaim the spoil. But that wasn't enough. It wanted more. And it took freely, with impunity.

The people gathered that morning were owners, or representatives of the owners, of 10 shorefront properties stretching from the Andrew Harding's Lane parking lot north 1,000 feet to the Mattaquason Point home of Anne Place, off Watch Hill Way. Within a few weeks the group would rally as a single, though often fractured, entity known as BREACH — Beach Reclamation Enactment Association of Chatham Harbor.

But on that particular Saturday, they were just 10 barely acquainted, alarmed homeowners in a quandary over how to protect their rapidly disappearing property.

Less than four months later, Anne Place and Ronald and Joan Wilson would be the only BREACH members present when the 41-year-old summer cottage of their neighbor, Judge Benjamin Galanti, slumped to the beach after more than two days of relentless pounding by the unforgiving Atlantic. It was the height of visibility for BREACH, Chatham and North Beach; the scene was replayed on the nightly news over and over again, like a nightmarish tape loop. In one sense, the events of that day succeeded in galvanizing those involved as only a disaster can. Yet it was hardly the end of either the erosion or the acrimonious battles between public and private interests, a complex, passionate, swirling miasma of bureaucrats, lawyers, judges, huge boulders and hundreds of thousands of dollars.

* * *

That first meeting, according to John Whelan, was emotional and disjointed. "Everybody went off on tangents, there was no direction," he said later. "Somebody wanted to put wrecked cars in front of their house, other people wanted to sink boats...Everybody had a solution, most of which would never have been allowed."

No one knew where to start. They had plenty of ideas, ranging from the credible to the incredible, but no context. How much control did the town, the state, the federal governments have over the protection of private property? What exactly could be done, legally? And could it be done in time to save their land and homes from becoming fish condominiums?

Step number one was to go to the Conservation Commission for advice and information, and that's what Whelan, Paul Galanti, son of property owner Benjamin Galanti, and a few others did on the evening of October 7.

Speaking near the end of the meeting, Whelan emotionally described the homeowners' plight, how the pace of erosion had quickened and consumed 40 to 50 feet of beach and dune in the space of a few weeks. "What can we do?" he implored. "Where do we go for help?"

The commissioners of course knew about the problem, but as chairman Douglas Wells explained to Whelan, there was little they could do. Under the state Wetlands Protection Act, and the town's own wetlands bylaw, an application to do work within 100 feet of the shore or

Top: Pre-break Holway Street. Wilson house is at left. Bottom: Holway Street to Andrew Harding's Lane, late 1988.

THE STORY OF CHATHAM'S NORTH BEACH

a wetlands, known as a "notice of intent," had to be filed before the commission, or property owners, could take any action. Except in the case of an emergency, and even that was strictly defined.

Advice, however, was free: Wells told Whelan and his band of property owners to get in touch with the Massachusetts Department of Environmental Quality Engineering, the agency which administers the wetlands act, and hire a coastal engineer to devise a "soft" solution, such as sandbags or beach nourishment. Under the law, a "hard" solution such as a rock seawall couldn't even be considered until something softer was attempted.

Even so, the property owners were put on notice that the host of permits required to do any work of consequence on the shore would take, at best, several weeks to secure. And it wasn't just local officials they had to deal with; DEQE had jurisdiction over anything done on the shore, and the state Division of Waterways and U.S. Army Corps of Engineers would be interested in any work done below the high water mark. Apply now, the message was, before the situation deteriorates further.

Galanti, an Indiana University law professor who numbered Dan Quayle among his past students, wasn't quite as reticent as Whelan. He told the commission that he was "a little upset with the attitude of the town" at its non-action concerning the parking lot at Andrew Harding's Lane. "We hope to do something. I hope the town will do something, without fear of liability," he said. "If not, they're asking us to sacrifice something that's been in our family for 50 years."

The following weekend BREACH met again, this time calling in an engineer named Joe Dorsett from Boston Survey Consultants, Inc., a firm based in Norwell and Mashpee. They showed him their problem; he told them to expect more erosion. But there were several "soft" options available, and Dorsett and BSC set about exploring.

Down the beach, the southeast corner of the Andrew Harding's Lane parking lot had been undermined and collapsed, leaving a hole eight feet wide by 20 feet long. Tides regularly reached up and over the eastern edge of the pavement, and the selectmen agreed to close half the parking lot to the public. Holway Street was totally closed off to public access; more than 30 feet had been shorn off the end since September, exposing a catch basin formerly well inland.

Appearing at a crowded selectmen's meeting on October 13, Dr. Giese reiterated his June recommendation that 50 feet of pavement be ripped up from the Andrew Harding's Lane parking lot and an artificial dune be built because it was still the spot most out of equilibrium with the system. The dune that would normally be absorbing the sea's energy was absent, leaving migrating sand with nothing to adhere to, the scientist said. Waves would continue to pound the shore until shoals built up offshore, something not likely to happen again until the next summer.

North Beach continued to contract, as did its estranged southern section. The breach was now more than three quarters of a mile wide from dune to dune.

Officials were split over what to do about the asphalt at Andrew Harding's Lane. Police Chief Barry Eldredge and Highway Surveyor Gilbert Borthwick favored leaving things as they were; the selectmen anguished over barring the public from access to the shore through the town landing; the ConCom, shellfish constable, waterways and fishing industry representatives wanted the broken tarmac out, for the rationale espoused by Giese as well as for public and navigational safety. Pieces of broken parking lot were beginning to show up below the water line.

Eventually, the town fathers voted to hire another division of BSC to devise some sort of soft measure to protect the parking lot. Their attention was still on potential liability, but now the focus had changed: If the erosion continued to progress, it would breach the parking lot and flood the low-lying areas to the west, destroying a wetland, inundating septic systems and flooding homes. Once again, the prospect of liability reared its ugly, litigious head. Was the town responsible if the erosion reached so far back that property was destroyed and houses had to be evacuated? There was quite a bit of pressure for the selectmen to do something about the parking lot. The answer suggested by Town Counsel Bruce Gilmore was to contact the area homeowners and ask them to sign a release, holding the town harmless in the eventuality that whatever was done at Andrew Harding's Lane backfired.

Along the shore interesting items were beginning to show up. The scouring currents unearthed — or unsanded — a trove of junk: old washing machines, antique glass and bottles, telephone poles (standing upright), bricks, old bottles, petrified trees and a meadow bank ledge that was probably thousands of years old.

Metal detectors and entire families digging huge pits in the low beach were common sights. For a short time the end of Andrew

Harding's Lane resembled the site of an archeological excavation. It was rare, but there were some real treasures among the junk, including a Revolutionary War-era pistol. Some of the junk came from dumps said to exist along the shoreline at one time. Some of the debris was said to have come from the house built at the foot of Mistover Lane by "Good" Walter Eldredge from bits and pieces of shipwrecks and flotsam he scouted out. It was known as "The Shipwreck House" and was bulldozed by the town when Good Walter died in the late 1950s.

An interesting bit of Chatham lore: the distinction between "Good" Walter Eldredge and the equally famous but unrelated "Wicked" Walter Eldredge reportedly came from Andrew Harding himself, who, during the late 1800s and early 1900s, ran a general store on the street that bears his name. It was a popular gathering spot for the men of the village, who would sit on the bench out front and crack jokes about passersby.

Harding never really minded the store much; he depended upon his customers to leave their money on the counter, which he'd collect at the end of the day. But he had trouble keeping the two Walter Eldredges straight. So he began calling the one who always paid his bills on time "Good" Walter, and the other, who was consistently late in paying, "Wicked" Walter. The latter even wrote a book, "Memoirs of Wicked Walter," about the men of Scrabbletown.

October 30 was a warm, sparkling autumn day, disturbed only by a brisk breeze escaping off the water. Near low tide, at the foot of the amputated Holway Street, members of the Conservation Commission and BREACH, which had adopted that publicity-perfect acronym a week earlier, gathered for an onsite hearing at the request of Peter Mason, whose mother was homeowner Ann Place. Seventy feet of beach in front of the Place homestead had been claimed, leaving beach stairs dangling in midair.

A three-tier system of sandbags, stacked tightly like bricks, along the entire stretch of beach, was proposed by BREACH. And they wanted to do it now. This was an emergency, they said, a conclusion with which members of the ConCom concurred. But in the course of the discussions on the beach, Mason said the commission should ignore the sandbag request and instead give BREACH emergency authorization to install a 1,000-foot windrow of boulders along the beach to break the destructive force of incoming waves. Only with a hard solution like rocks could BREACH members be assured of protecting their

THE PLAYERS

Barry Eldredge — Chatham's chief of police at the time of the breakthrough.

Peter Ford — Chatham harbormaster in 1987.

Paul Galanti — University of Indiana law professor whose family owned the first home to fall victim to erosion.

Dr. Graham Giese — Woods Hole Oceanographic Institution scientist whose study of the Nauset barrier beach system predicted the 1987 breakthrough.

Bruce Gilmore — Chatham's town attorney.

Peter Mason — Fast-talking son of property owner Ann Place, he tried to push his self-engineered erosion solutions through the BREACH group and often alienated officials with his blunt criticism.

Alfred and Evelyn Nelson — Little Beach property owners who carried on the fight to protect their homes from erosion into the 1990s.

William Riley — Local attorney who represented BREACH in the early days of erosion.

Nicholas Soutter — Wellesley attorney who represented several erosion victims. His aggressiveness didn't endear him to local officials, but his tenacity was admirable. He ended up taking two cases to the U.S. Supreme Court, the only time Chatham-related cases have gone before the nation's highest court.

Douglas Wells — Conservation Commission chairman at the time of the breakthrough, he tried to balance compassion for homeowners with the need to enforce state and local wetlands laws.

John Whelan — Holway Street property owner and one of the first to see the effect of erosion first-hand. He served as spokesman for the BREACH group in its early dealings with the town.

Ronald and Joan Wilson — BREACH members whose Andrew Harding's Lane home was lost to erosion.

Andrew Young — Chatham selectman and former conservation commission member.

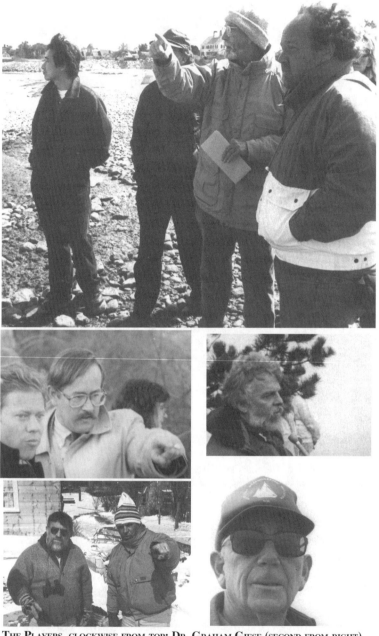

THE PLAYERS, CLOCKWISE FROM TOP: DR. GRAHAM GIESE (SECOND FROM RIGHT) AND CONSERVATION COMMISSION MEMBER JOHN GIEGER; PETER MASON; DOUGLAS WELLS; JOHN WHELAN (RIGHT) SHOWS EROSION DAMAGE TO DR. ORRIN PILKEY; ANDREW YOUNG WITH STATE ENVIRONMENTAL SECRETARY JOHN DEVILLARS.

BREAKTHROUGH

homes and land. Processes in place elsewhere to curb erosion, such as fishing nets and artificial reefs, wouldn't work here; the currents were too swift, the waves too large. Even though nothing in the way of erosion protection had yet been attempted, Mason claimed that "the soft solutions are costing money."

Despite Wells' repetition of the applicable section of the state and local laws, Mason pressed for approval of the row of rocks. "It's going beyond emergency steps," Wells replied; if a wall was what they ultimately wanted, they had better make application for one as quickly as possible. Meanwhile, a soft solution would at least buy time.

Mason wasn't satisfied and the following day fired off a handwritten letter to the commission and selectmen on BREACH stationery. Sandbags, the letter stated, would be too costly and susceptible to vandalism and wear by waves, ice and sun. "Our intense search for a solution...leads unquestionably to one answer: a continuous revetment of rock joining already existing areas of rock revetment in front of Chatham Light and Watch Hill, supplemented by sandbags." (The reference to rocks near Watch Hill applied to a scattering of granite and loose rocks at the foot of the bank, put there in the early decades of this century and uncovered by erosion.)

This dichotomy between rocks and sandbags (and later a BSC plan for a rolled filter cloth filled with sand, called a Longard tube) formed the nexus of the initial controversy between BREACH and the commission. It also marked Mason's active entry into the fray; he had come up with a catchy, public relations-savvy name for the group, and had been touting since early October something called "Mason Breach Control," which essentially called for building a breakwater and canal where the North Beach cut-through was and filling in the missing parts of the beach, the results being not unlike the plan the Army Corps had given up on in the early '70s.

Not a property owner himself, Mason represented his mother, whose home was originally owned by Marcellus Eldredge, the founder and builder of Chatham's town library, the Eldredge Public Library. Mason's letterhead read "creative engineering" and his personal calling card was a confusing jumble of run-on words announcing his proclivity in everything from public relations to architect; but nobody was quite sure exactly what he did for a living. A tall, good-looking man with salt and pepper hair and a neatly trimmed beard, Mason was followed everywhere by his German Shepherd, Styro, and, in the early months of the erosion, could often be found on the beach in the early morning chronicling the devastation with a video camera. He wasn't an engineer, despite the "viable" solutions he kept coming up with, but he was an effective and powerful public speaker and gradually assumed the role of chief spokesman for BREACH.

Many of those involved place much of the contention and obfuscation of the next few months at Mason's feet. It certainly began with his insistence on rocks, at all costs, despite the acceptance by some members of BREACH of the sandbag-tube methods of protection. Mason was responsible for bringing in some of the drama's key players early in 1988: Professor Jerome Connors, a civil engineer from the Massachusetts Institute of Technology, and Nicholas Soutter, an aggressive Wellesley attorney who instigated BREACH's $10 million lawsuit against the state, the first of many court actions precipitated by the North Beach breach.

Mason was in sharp contrast to Whelan, BREACH's other high-profile member, a local stockbroker and long-time resident who had moved into his Holway Street home in 1984. The neighborhood was home; his mother had lived in the house immediately to the west, and many of the people in the area were like family. Along with Pam Butler Roberts, whose mother Effie Butler owned the second house south of Holway Street, Whelan had initially galvanized the erosion victims and served as principal spokesman. He was the person I always called for background or comments for a newspaper story.

Of the other BREACH members, Ronald and Joan Wilson were perhaps the most visible. Their cottage, the third north of Andrew Harding's Lane, had been built in the 1940s by Joan's father, and was gutted by a fire in the winter of 1987. An engineer in his home state of Florida, Ron Wilson often seemed frustrated at not being able to help the group out in his chosen profession, since he wasn't a registered professional in Massachusetts. Yet he and his wife made frequent trips to Chatham from their Florida home, and their son David took up residence to look after the family's interests.

Roger and Doris Chapdelaine, whose home was next to Whelan's, ran an antique store in downtown Chatham during the summer. The property directly south of Whelan's was owned by the Whiting family, which remained distant from the whole problem save in times of crisis — such as major storms — when a family member put in an appearance to save their cottage from ultimate destruction either by nature or the town. Grace Coxhead owned the house immediately south of Holway Street. Between the Butler and Wilson land was an empty lot owned by Winifred Lear, Whelan's cousin.

Judge Benjamin Galanti lived in Lodi, New Jersey, and was described by Whelan as "the most upright guy I ever knew." Whelan and Paul Galanti, the judge's son, grew up together summers. As teenagers they worked together in a sporting goods store in downtown Chatham. Frederick Rolfe, the southernmost member of BREACH, lived in western Massachusetts. His cottage was reportedly the first summer home built in the area, in the early years of the century. It was purchased by Rolfe's father in the 1940s.

Being spokesman for such a diverse and far-ranging group wasn't easy. Pam Butler Roberts helped hold things together, according to Whelan, by using her computer expertise to keep track of names, addresses and finances. But she lived in California, so Whelan initially took on the role he said was like "being the leader of a Latin American country. You've no idea what's going on in the outlying districts, you have no idea what the heck they're doing. The only thing you know is what's going on right here this minute. That's all I really knew."

The first official designation of an emergency and the work permit which went along with it came from the Conservation Commission on November 19, after BSC submitted a plan to lay a double row of sand-filled fabric tubes (Longard tubes) along 900 feet of private beach. Peggy Fantozzi, the BSC engineer working for the town, suggested to the selectmen that the tube be extended across Andrew Harding's Lane, providing a unified front against the continuing erosive destruction. If the town agreed to donate 5,000 cubic yards of sand to fill the tubes, the cost to both BREACH and Chatham would total about $156,000, reasonable given the protection it would afford.

No one ever pretended that the tube, which eventually gained the derogatory and easier to remember label "yankee kielbasa," was a permanent solution. Its purpose was to buy time, to at least slow down the erosion that was carving out tens of feet of dune and banking weekly. But the erosion remained the only activity on the shoreline. In late November both Wilson and Mason said the $145 per foot Longard tube cost was too high. Wilson pushed for sandbags, Mason for rocks. Sandbags won out, for a short time, over the Longard tube, according to Whelan, although Mason continued to dissent (he referred to the Longard tube as the "Chatham condom"). Ninety 20-foot long filter cloth sandbags were ordered from a Florida company.

Filling the bags with sand proved another obstacle. Water and sand had to be pumped into the huge bags via hydraulic equipment; Whelan said attempts were made to hire a cement truck to mix the slurry, but no contractor was willing to risk it. Contractor George Viprino slapped together a huge funnel-topped contraption to do the job, but only a few bags were filled, and placed in front of the Galanti cottage, by now obviously the structure in most imminent danger. The entire sandbag-tube episode was labeled a "false step" by Whelan.

The southern tip of North Beach continued to curl back, 100 feet during one stormy weekend.

So it was back to rocks. At another Conservation Commission onsite meeting on December 3, Mason gave reasons why he believed the rock plan, now expanded from a windrow to an irregular revetment on top of filter cloth, was better than tubes or sandbags: The expected wave height in the harbor of up to eight feet was well above the Army Corps of Engineers' criteria for Longard tube long-term effectiveness, which was maxed out in a wave environment of five feet; tubes and sandbags would be nearly impossible to remove, reposition or repair once on the beach, and would foster wave reflection and thus scouring of the ocean floor immediately seaward of the beach; and it would take too long to install, up to 40 days. Rocks, on the other hand, would dissipate wave energy and filter cloth beneath would trap sand; they could also be moved quickly and, perhaps more importantly, were cheaper.

BSC was fired, and EIT Engineering, a firm owned by MIT professor Jerome Connors with offices in Cambridge and Sagamore, was hired at Mason's instigation. A letter echoing Mason's sentiments about rocks was signed by most BREACH members and delivered to the commission and DEQE's Southeast Regional headquarters in Lakeville.

By now Conservation Commission members had lost confidence in BREACH. Not only had the group procrastinated in installing interim erosion control measures that had been given quick emergency approval, nothing in the way of an official request or notice of intent for anything beyond emergency measures had been forthcoming in the two months since they first approached the commission. As far as the commission was concerned, the firing of BSC didn't help BREACH, nor did Mason's continued chiding of the ConCom members for their opposition and perceived foot-dragging. For the commission, it was time to bring in the heavy guns.

Enter the Massachusetts DEQE, Coastal Zone Management Office, and the Division of Waterways. Representatives attended a pivotal meeting on the beach December 10, and gave BREACH members the harsh news that despite the tragic and extensive loss of property, a rock revetment was definitely out of the question.

Liz Kouloheras, wetlands chief from DEQE's Lakeville office, urged a temporary soft structure as a buffer to "get you through the winter while you look at a more long-term solution." She and Jeff Benoit of CZM spent most of the morning examining the composition of the eroded banks and bluffs from Rolfe's to Place's, concluding, in what was later to become a chief contention between the state and BREACH, that the landward bluffs of the four southernmost properties (Rolfe, Galanti, Wilson and Lear) were coastal dunes, while to the north were coastal banks.

The distinction was important, because under the wetlands act, engineered structures are not permitted, under any circumstances, on dunes, which are defined as shifting sand formations shaped by wind and wave action that contribute sediment to a dynamic coastal system. Banks, however, can host engineered structures provided they protect homes in existence before 1978, the year the applicable regulation was promulgated. Banks, composed mostly of glacial outwash, are generally accepted to be more permanent than dunes.

Jack Clarke, CZM's Cape representative, stood back during most of the meeting, his arms folded, listening intently to the debate. Later, he said engineered structures like seawalls and revetments usually throw a coastal system out of equilibrium, diverting damaging erosion to another section of shore. They simply shift the problem elsewhere. Unless the entire eastern shoreline of Chatham were armored, a rock revetment could cause major damage, as much as the present erosion, and that was something no one wanted to see. If that happened, Mason argued, the rocks would be removed. Not likely, countered Benoit; once the rocks are on the beach, he said, "the chance of their coming out is nil." Sandbags or tubes, on the other hand, could be split and their contents spilled harmlessly on the beach should they prove damaging or ineffective.

Both state and local officials categorically denied Mason's rock proposal. Aside from matters of bureaucratic regulation and geology, they didn't think much of the proposed revetment design. The two-ton boulder size would be too small to prevent shifting of a revetment; the toe (or foundation) of the revetment wasn't deep enough to provide stability; the engineering was simply poor.

Kouloheras told Mason point-blank, "We're not going to allow an emergency structure that wouldn't normally be allowed under the regulations."

Since nothing was being done by BREACH, the town could not go ahead with the plan BSC had come up with for an artificial dune across the Andrew Harding's Lane parking lot; there was nothing to tie it into on the northern end, and it would therefore be ineffective.

A lot of criticism was leveled against the town fathers for taking no action to protect town property, and, by that inaction, endangering surrounding private land. While town government isn't known for its fleetness, certainly the equal procrastination of BREACH is as much to blame. That Board of Selectmen had further considerations: A new system of government composed of five part-time members had replaced the three-member full-time board in May; Jim Lindstrom, the executive secretary — or town administrator — had only been on the job since February. Getting their act together proved to be more difficult than originally thought. Only two members of the former board remained to provide continuity, and another, arguably more important issue took up most of the summer: the loss and subsequent re-vote of a tax override ballot , without which town government would have been crippled. A temporary freeze on spending delayed the Andrew Harding's Lane project, yet the board continued to accommodate the BREACH group at weekly meetings and kept in constant contact, through Lindstrom, with property owners in the shore area.

Another factor, according to Andrew Young, a former selectman who was a member of the Conservation Commission at the time, was uncertainty over just how long the erosion would continue. Dr. Giese predicted, and it was generally accepted in scientific circles, that South Beach would gradually break up and migrate west, exposing even more of the mainland to the direct fury of the Atlantic. The erosive efforts along the comparatively small section of shoreline from Andrew Harding's Lane to Holway Street "pale in comparison to the prospects of erosion and flooding that could occur over the evolution of the break," Young warned.

Money was just as much a concern for the town as it was to BREACH members, given the strained purse strings engendered under a Massachusetts law, Proposition 2½ , which capped increases in property taxes without special votes. Closing a town landing was also something selectmen did not do lightly; access to the town's shoreline, the lifeblood of both the fishing and tourist industries, was limited enough already. Closing Holway Street and Andrew Harding's Lane would only exacerbate the situation for beachgoers, boaters, fin and shellfishermen. They wanted to protect their options and not abandon the landings, since the long term prognosis continued to be that the beach would someday build up again.

More than 100 feet eroded in front of the Rolfe, Galanti and Wilson properties between September and late December. High tide regularly reached up and touched a porch in front of the boathouse attached to Galanti's cottage, and it was totally undermined by the week before Christmas, hanging suspended in the air as the marbly froth of the breakers froze on the surrounding beachgrass. Sand that had been dumped in front of the Coxhead and Butler homes earlier in the month was gone within a few weeks. The bluff was 13 feet high and steep, and it didn't take long for the pounding waves to expose a septic system, which prompted Health Agent Jane Evans to declare the house uninhabitable.

About this time things got a little crazy.

BREACH hired local attorney William Riley and on December 21 he went to Barnstable Superior Court to ask for a temporary restraining order against the town, state and federal governments so they could not stop the construction of Mason's temporary revetment. In her decision, Judge Elizabeth Dolan granted the request, but required a $100,000 bond to insure the rocks' removal if a subsequent hearing reversed the order. A sketch plan by EIT showed two-ton rocks placed atop filter cloth and built up to an elevation of twelve feet (about eight feet above the beach level), along with a series of groins perpendicular to the shore constructed of sand-filled Dura-bags (a brand of sandbags measuring two by five feet and weighing a ton when filled).

Angry at having been bypassed, frustrated at having only a few hours to prepare for the hearing, town and state officials lashed out at the BREACH group, saying the escalating erosion was as much a product of the property owners' inaction and failure to take advantage of emergency permits — issued in early November — as the ocean raged through the North Beach break. Their methods were also criticized. Court action normally wasn't sought until after the administrative process was exhausted; BREACH hadn't even submitted a formal notice of intent. If everyone who wanted to skirt the established process went running to court, what then was the purpose of protective regulations, the town argued, no doubt bruised by the threatened loss of control. This was the second time a homeowner along Chatham Harbor had ignored environmental regulatory agencies and applied directly to court for relief; but BREACH went further than Maurice Hartley by naming the state and federal governments in the injunction, thus sweeping aside virtually all impediments to their "ultimate solution" to erosion.

The plan, unlike any that had been proposed to date, particularly concerned the Conservation Commission because of the inclusion of groins, or breakwaters extending perpendicular to the revetment. Never before had jetties like these been mentioned in connection with erosion protection. The town, in the past, had been forced to accept groins along the Nantucket Sound shoreline, which became irregular due to uneven erosion and accretion. Those groins in turn prompted several homeowners to build intrusive, ecologically damaging seawalls.

The day after the injunction was issued, trucks carrying huge boulders rolled into town. Dumped below the seaward edge of the disintegrating Andrew Harding's Lane parking lot, they were plucked one by one with a front end loader and distributed along the shoreline. Crowds watched the action from early morning till sunset.

But instead of being placed against the foot of the bluffs, as the plans indicated, the rocks were strewn haphazardly along the shore several yards seaward. There seemed to be no cohesiveness, logic or "structure" to the placement. Although members of the BREACH group were satisfied and told the press the rocks were stopping erosion, environmental officials disagreed. In fact, shortly after the rocks appeared on the shore, the level of the beach dropped by several feet, mainly from the Wilson property south. It was obvious the haphazard placement of the rocks was exacerbating erosion.

The state had its day in court on December 30, when Judge Dolan presided over a daylong hearing on the injunction at Barnstable Superior Court. The room was liberally peppered with news reporters and lawyers, BREACH and ConCom members, and more lawyers. Madelyn Morris, an assistant attorney general for environmental affairs, squared off against Riley, known for his facile, sometimes sarcastic work before local boards and commissions on behalf of clients ranging from retired homeowners to major developers. The rock wall, Riley argued, was "necessary to provide protection to property owners during the lengthy permitting process." Morris countered with the dune defense: "As a general rule, engineered structures aren't allowed" on coastal dunes. Bruce Gilmore, the town's attorney, placed the blame at the feet of BREACH for not taking advantage of the emergency permits when they were issued.

Dolan admitted her previous decision to allow the rocks had been somewhat hasty, based on the possibility of "dire and visual consequences of immediate harm" to several homes. She in effect tried to back out of the situation, indicating she felt the court did not belong in what was essentially a technical, scientific dispute between environmental officials and homeowners. In an interlocutory order issued January 4, 1988, the judge declined to uphold the injunction. Instead, she ordered the rocks removed from the Galanti, Rolfe, Wilson and Lear properties (all on coastal dunes) within 40 days. The rest of the rocks could stay in place, but the property owners were ordered to make formal application to the town and state, which the town and state agreed to put on a "fast track" under an accelerated schedule set up by the court. Both sides hailed the decision as a victory.

Finally, on January 15, after months of exhortations by local officials, BREACH submitted a formal notice of intent, essentially asking permission to build the rock wall already begun along the shoreline.

But it was already too late, at least for the three southernmost properties. The ocean whipped itself into a fury and, coupled with an 11½-foot perigee tide, pounded the hell out of the Galanti, Rolfe and Wilson properties for two weeks in mid January, completely ignoring the loose rocks that had been placed on the beach in apparent hopes that sand would build up between them and the base of the dunes.

The base of the dune lay at the foundation of the Galanti cottage by Tuesday, January 19. The boathouse porch had already broken off; the boathouse itself now jutted out from the rest of the house in apparent defiance of gravity. Riley asked for the commission's approval to bring in more rocks. Town officials, unsure how to treat the request in light of the court order, sought clarification from Judge Dolan.

Commission members gathered that Tuesday and watched waves break underneath the Galanti boathouse and gnaw on the cottage's foundation. Chunks of compact sand surrendered to the sea, which reached up to the floorboards. Why was the revetment never completed according to plan, they wanted to know. Speaking for his clients, Riley answered, "We were never allowed to finish the job."

As the parties parried, the sea prepared for the final assault on the Galanti cottage. Lights, camera, action: This was the week that put Chatham on the media map.

* * *

Early morning, Wednesday, January 20. More rock-filled trucks crept into town. Given the court order, Chief Eldredge wasn't sure if he should let the rocks near the beach. Gilmore advised him to deny the vehicles access to the town landings at Andrew Harding's Lane and Holway Street.

The trucks found their way to the beach anyway, down Andrew Harding's Lane and onto the Wilson property via a driveway/access road. At about 10:30 that morning, the first load of rocks was dumped over the bluff and onto the beach a few feet south of the Wilson cottage. It was precarious work; more than 170 feet of beach had disappeared and the house was nearly as close to the edge as its neighbor — within a few feet, actually. The fragile land shook as the rocks crashed to the beach below.

No one would say who gave George Viprino the OK to dump the rocks. Trucks continued to arrive all day long, despite the issuance by Judge Dolan of a clarification specifically prohibiting the addition of rocks to the dune area.

Next door, John Whelan began removing valuables and potentially harmful chemicals and paints from the Galanti cottage. Whelan, John Ottow and Dennis Martin — local landscapers — moved as much furniture as they could, trucking it to town-owned property near the Chatham airport for temporary storage. The scene was "like a preliminary death knell," Whelan said later.

All day long news reporters, photographers and television camera crews held a grim vigil. I was one of them, but I was a familiar figure on the beach and had been making almost daily visits since December to chart the progression of the erosion. Most of the new arrivals were television crews outfitted with huge quantities of expensive equipment, live remote trucks and the requisite talking heads, who persisted in referring to Andrew Harding's Beach as North Beach and thrust microphones in the face of anyone who looked even vaguely official. It was the perfect photo opportunity, excessively visual, dramatic, and emotional. BREACH people made their pitch on the evening news, ripping the town up and down for failing to prevent the impending disaster.

THE GALANTI HOUSE RESTS ON THE BEACH AFTER BEING UNDERMINED BY EROSION.

AN EXCAVATOR IS USED TO DEMOLISH THE GALANTI HOUSE TO PREVENT IT FROM BREAKING APART AND THE PIECES BECOMING A HAZARD TO NAVIGATION.

THE STORY OF CHATHAM'S NORTH BEACH

The day was cold and damp, but that didn't deter crowds of on-lookers from parking on Hallett Lane and lower Main Street and walking down Andrew Harding's Lane to catch a glimpse of the sea splashing against the weathered shingles of the cottage. During low tide police allowed the curious to roam the beach, but when the waves began to crash toward the bluffs, a barricade was erected and people stood, often five or six deep, a hundred yards back from the beach. There wasn't much to see from that vantage point, but that didn't stem the flow. "It was almost sadistic," Whelan commented afterwards. "People standing around waiting for a house to fall."

The next day, things went from crazy to downright insane.

The media arrived early, positioning themselves for what seemed to be the inevitable. During the night the tide had worked over Galanti's cottage and it was clear it would not survive the day. BREACH members and a cadre of supporters, carrying signs and handing out leaflets, paraded in front of the cameras. A depressing, chilling drizzle began to fall.

Emotion was as thick as the damp, wintry air. Tension between town officials on the scene and BREACH members built during the course of the morning, neither speaking, until someone spray painted a piece of plywood with the words "Doug Wells Memorial" and tacked it to the gray clapboards of the cottage.

It was a low point in relations between the two sides. Wells, an intelligent, direct man who'd developed a thick skin in his years on the Conservation Commission, was visibly hurt by the slight, and even though the sign was quickly removed by Mason and Wilson and apologies were offered, the damage was done. It had been captured on video and by news photographs and would be seen by countless people.

At about 12:50 p.m., as a TV reporter interviewed Wilson in the eroding space between cottages, the battered Galanti house shuddered, creaked, and tipped toward the beach. Its chimney toppled like a set of child's blocks and, as a final, decisive wave crashed around it, the house slumped the rest of the way to the beach and settled at a 45-degree angle.

What everyone had feared had finally happened: The breach in North Beach had claimed a victim, its first in more than 100 years. Wilson stood staring at the husk of his neighbor's cottage and said only that he was "very depressed."

Instead of quelling the frenzy that had been building, the surrender of the Galanti cottage, and its replay countless times on local and national news shows, whipped up people even more. Crowds grew thicker, officials flocked to the scene to secure the premises for safety. Health Agent Jane Evans ordered the septic system pumped so waste wouldn't pollute the harbor; Harbormaster Peter Ford wondered aloud who would clean up the debris already beginning to break off the cottage and float down the harbor. Helicopters carrying television cameras and news photographers whizzed by as demonstrators flashed placards exclaiming "Chatham won't let us save our homes."

The episode was repeated over and over again on the Hyannis, Boston and Providence television stations; a spot even made it on to the Cable News Network. "It was Andy Warhol's `famous-for-15-minutes' bit," comments Whelan. A few days before, a huge storm had destroyed a number of buildings in Redondo Beach, California. The damage in Chatham was much less, but the coverage was equal to or greater than the California storm.

Nicholas Soutter, the attorney hired by BREACH on Mason's recommendation, made his first appearance that day, either by chance or design. An abrasive, audacious and high-pressure trial lawyer from the upscale Boston suburb of Wellesley, Soutter was apparently brought in to add some legal muscle to BREACH; the scheme was that he would handle the court work, Riley the permit hearings. Two weeks later he filed, on behalf of BREACH, a $10 million civil lawsuit against the state, claiming that the loss of a total of three acres of property and the deprivation of use of the homes due to shoreline conditions were attributable to negligence on the part of the state agencies. In the suit, "erosion" became "flooding," and cautious inaction became the taking of land without compensation. Specifically cited was the lack of action at Andrew Harding's Lane. Soutter said its very creation in 1955 helped heighten the erosion by throwing the system out of kilter. But the town was not named in the suit. BREACH, said Soutter, was "holding out the olive branch to them." But it didn't help BREACH's image with the state. Officials confided in private that the suit resolved them to hold the group to the strict letter of the law. No bend, no give, no more Mr. Nice Regulator.

A Harvard graduate who spoke five languages, Soutter was to prove one of the longest-lasting participants in this drama, continuing to represent shoreline property owners well into the new century. No one ever questioned his tenacity; he brought two Chatham erosion cases to the U.S. Supreme Court and, still undaunted, continued to represent the Wilson and Rolfe families, whose homes were long gone.

Back on that fateful Thursday, Steve Rolfe arrived to remove his family's possessions just in time to watch his neighbor's cottage fall into the water. It made him sick, he said; he hadn't been aware that the situation had deteriorated so quickly. In fact, it was only because of a news story the previous evening that he and his wife, Deborah, realized they'd better do something about the family cottage, and quick.

A week later, after wrecking crews had demolished the Galanti cottage by order of the selectmen, Whelan mused over the episode.

"I found the whole thing unfortunate," he said. "We saw a house go into the water. We felt terrible, terrible frustration, because we felt our hands were tied.

"No one actually felt this had anything to do with vindictiveness on the part of Doug Wells. We've all been aware the commission's done its best." Later, in an interview in his home, Whelan gave both Wells and senior commission member Alice Hiscock credit for being on the scene that day and for "taking the crap."

"They handle this job with a tremendous amount of dignity," he said. "I don't always agree with Alice, but I respect her because she has the nerve of her convictions."

The reality of the situation also came home to many others in the neighborhood. Elwyn and Ruth Perry lived in the oldest house in the area, built in 1807, situated right behind the Galanti lot, at the time about eight feet from the receding bluff.

They'd lived there since 1968, and had begun slowly packing some belongings in case they were forced to vacate. "We have a little bit of common sense and realize we might not be able to stay," Mrs. Perry said. "But we're going to stay as long as we can."

All of the BREACH homeowners had federal flood insurance. A few days after the disastrous plunge, President Ronald Reagan signed into law a housing bill that carried a provision extending the coverage to erosion damage. Homeowners who elected to move structures out of harm's way would be eligible to receive 40 percent of the building's value; if the structure was torn down, 110 percent of the value would be paid, but the land could never be built upon again.

A week after the Galanti house succumbed, the first hearing was held on the group's formal application for a seawall amid a crush of cameras, reporters and nearly 100 onlookers. During the three-hour session, Professor Connors and Dr. John Millman, a senior scientist at the Woods Hole Oceanographic Institute, presented detailed descriptions of the barrier beach system and the composition of the landforms of the BREACH properties. The issue of dune versus bank once again became a critical factor; if they could prove the four southernmost properties were coastal banks, not coastal dunes, it was likely a revetment would be approved for the entire length of the beach.

After postponing the hearing for a week so Millman could obtain soil samples, the Conservation Commission acquiesced and voted to

MEMBERS OF **BREACH** AND SUPPORTERS MAKE THEIR CASE BEFORE NEWS HELICOPTERS THE DAY THE GALANTI HOUSE SUCCUMBED.

approve the entire wall by a 5-1 vote (Alice Hiscock dissented). In the preamble to the order of conditions, Wells wrote that the embankment on the Rolfe, Galanti, Wilson and Lear properties were "so wasted by the shock of the Nauset Beach break that they are simply unable to perform the functions" of a dune. BREACH had won a round.

But it was a guarded victory; a number of state agencies still had to pass on the plan, as did the Army Corps of Engineers. The interlocutory order was still in place, and the rocks had not been removed from the dune area nor had the interim wall been completed according to plan.

Meanwhile, the Rolfes elected to move their house after the tides continued to encroach, undermining the foundation and causing the porch to collapse. The move took the cottage past the hauntingly empty Galanti lot, to the rear of the Wilson property, where it remained until October 1988. Effie Butler initiated the process of moving her home, but it was lifted off its foundation and placed on temporary supports until it was too late to do anything about it, and it was finally demolished in 1991.

DEQE's overruling of the commission on the dune issue doomed the Rolfe and Wilson homes, and the failure of the Butler and Coxhead families to complete revetments cemented their homes' fate as well.

By February 1988 there was a 900-foot stretch of open, scarred shoreline where two houses once stood. Late in the month a contractor was hired to rearrange the 7,000 tons of rocks on the beach into a cohesive wall. But instead of starting at the toe of the bluffs, the rocks were piled, 10 to 15 feet high, about 30 feet from the bank, creating a sort of waterfront tunnel. Walking behind it at high tide, a person could peer out through the wide chinks at the ocean trying to desperately get through. The irregular structure stretched from Place's to Wilson's, where a crib-like configuration was built and filled with sand to recreate at least some of the frontage lost to the sea. Eventually, sand was dumped behind the entire length of the wall; as the ocean continued to batter it, however, the sediment seeped out from between the boulders. Hackles were raised among fishermen when the sand, yellow-rust in color, started showing up on shoals and sandbars throughout the harbor.

While BREACH decided to appeal the DEQE ruling, the state and town agreed to let the judge's order for removal of the dune-facing rocks lie dormant, at least until the entire administrative process was completed.

BREAKTHROUGH

The prospect of more lawsuits soon popped up again, this time directed at the BREACH group. While climbing on the rocks, a 10-year-old boy suffered cuts and bruises when the unstable rocks shifted and trapped his leg. Chief Eldredge and Deputy Police Chief Wayne Love happened to be nearby, posting no trespassing signs on the Galanti land, when they heard the loud thump of settling rock and a scream. They looked at each other, horrified. While Eldredge called the rescue squad, Love managed to lever the rocks loose enough to pull the boy free. It wasn't long afterwards that "stay off the rocks" signs popped up everywhere. Not many were discouraged, however, as a small but steady stream of sightseers continued along the shoreline daily during the winter. By spring, there were nearly as many people on the beach on weekends as sunbathed there the previous summer.

Between February and May things had slowed. The wall did protect most of the properties, but there were clear side effects. Immediately south of the wall, waves gouged out 50 more feet from the Galanti and Rolfe lots. Galanti's septic system, which had been on the landward side of the cottage, was exposed in the cut-away dune and crumbled to the beach in mid-April. Once accommodating more than 50 cars, the parking lot at Andrew Harding's Lane was a pile of sand and asphalt, hammered into small chunks and distributed downdrift toward Lighthouse Beach by the intense harbor currents. It looked as if it had been hit by a small bomb. Tons of sand were uselessly dumped there until the selectmen decided to remove the last five or six feet of pavement. The huge berm built by Gibby Borthwick to keep the ocean off the interior lowlands held, for the moment.

State waterways officials worked the BREACH plan in the meantime, coming up with a significantly larger revetment design, 20 feet high and 48 feet wide at the base, with huge boulders as anchors and containing more than 20,000 tons of rock. This was to become the standard Chatham revetment design, the template for an eventual 29 walls.

Projected costs soared, from an estimated $400 per foot to nearly $1,000. Soutter immediately fired off a number of invectives, calling the design "The Great Wall of Chatham." Robert Weaver, EIT's project coordinator, issued press releases assuring everyone that the new design was a cooperative effort between his firm, BREACH and the state.

Soutter was, however, "desperately hopeful" that the state would change its mind and allow the original design. Wilson said that as an

ROCKS SCATTERED ALONG THE SHORE FAILED TO SAVE THE GALANTI HOUSE, WHICH CAN BE SEEN LYING ON THE SHORE AT THE TOP OF THE PHOTO. HOLWAY STREET IS AT THE BOTTOM.

BREAKTHROUGH

engineer, he wouldn't advise a client to build the structure as approved. BREACH's underplaying of the state's plan had one overriding motivation: money. The 500 feet of wall they could legally build would cost more than half a million dollars. They had already spent more than $250,000. Legal fees amounted to at least $30,000 of that. There remained doubts as to whether the entire wall would ever be built, since both the Galanti and Rolfe properties were, by April, more than half eaten away, and it was doubtful they'd be willing to shell out thousands of dollars to protect an empty lot, which might even be underwater soon.

Chatham was also emptying its pockets, although to a lesser extent. BSC's engineered plan, never implemented, cost $3,000, and legal fees amounted to more than $3,600. Overtime for police officers stationed at Andrew Harding's Lane and Holway Street came to more than $3,500. If the 38 hours Gibby Borthwick spent removing 90 truckloads of asphalt from the beach and replacing it with 1,837 cubic yards of sand was equated to private contractor rates, it would have cost the town more than $9,000.

Action on the legal front continued full blast. The state asked for and was granted dismissal of the $10 million suit. Soutter called the action a declaration of war and vowed to sue Chatham. Town Counsel Bruce Gilmore quipped that "the legal entanglements are becoming as dynamic as the changes in the shorefront." BREACH fired Riley; he didn't get along with Soutter, and vice versa. Riley later played both sides of the fence, representing a group of homeowners protesting another proposal for a seawall just north of Ann Place's property, as well as two Morris Island property owners worried about the erosion of their million-dollar lots.

As if spreading itself into a broad, mocking grin, the breach now left a mile-wide opening for the Atlantic's punchlines.

At the next Town Meeting, voters refused to spend any money to protect town-owned property from Andrew Harding's Lane south. It wasn't hard to sense the mood of the people: Let nature take its course.

If the town was at fault for sticking to the wait-and-see philosophy, BREACH, too, inflicted a number of its own wounds. They vacillated, they were inconsistent, they failed to heed well-intentioned advice; they even failed to show up at Town Meeting to move an article for public funds to pay for the 30 feet of revetment across Holway Street, an article they had proposed and written. A number of questions lingered unanswered, months after the fact, and the Conservation Commission seemed to be taking the brunt of the criticism. Perhaps the fact that BREACH lasted only a few months speaks as to which was the more stable organization.

A new group formed shortly thereafter, calling itself S.O.S., "Save Our Shores." Led by Mason and other former BREACH members, their friends and supporters, the group tried to enlist state and federal help in getting a short-term dredging program going, so they could benefit from the tons of sand to be dug up from the harbor bottom, much of it eroded from their own properties.

A meeting was held in Boston in early May with all the bigwigs — Army Corps, DEQE, Waterways, Federal Emergency Management Agency, State Senator Paul Doane, and a representative of Congressman Studds. Mason was incredulous that the public wouldn't be allowed to attend, especially BREACH and SOS, who, after all, got the ball rolling in the first place (so he claimed). The Attorney General's office had made the decision to close the meeting based on litigation by the property owners. It seemed perfectly simple: even a notably illogical entity like state government knows when not to invite the fox into the chicken coop.

In late May a public "breach summit" was held in Chatham. It was an unremarkable meeting at which the various players agreed to what they'd agreed to earlier in the private session: to work together to expedite harbor dredging and put together a long-range management plan the town could refer to over the next 50 years, as North Beach and the harbor continue to change.

Despite the widely-held perception, even among Chatham residents, that shoreline homeowners are wealthy to the last, some BREACH members couldn't afford to build revetments, or for their own reasons never followed through after permits were issued. While the elements took the Rolfe, Wilson and Galanti houses, it was a failure to act, for whatever purpose — financial or otherwise — that spelled the end for the Butler and Coxhead homes. And their lack of action had repercussions. Hazel Witherbee, who lived behind the Coxhead house, was forced to move out of her home after it was severely damaged by two major storms in 1991 and 1992. The Coxhead wall had never been built, and the house was long gone.

Whelan affirmed his right to protect his property, but rejected any intimation of public financial support. "If you want to enjoy living at the beach, you've got to pay for your own protection. If you choose not to, there's always someone willing to buy it."

Town officials probably could have been more accommodating to the homeowners; they could have relieved pressure on themselves by bringing the state in at an earlier point. But personalities became entangled in the winter's miasma of events, and Whelan regrets that. He has kind words for local officials, especially members of the Conservation Commission, who were "in a difficult position."

"I've known some of these people for 30 years. At first, some of the homeowners thought, here we have a major asset, and our friends and neighbors are preventing us from protecting it. It was a learning process on our side, and the commission's too."

Will he continue living on the shore, in a home less than 50 feet from the ocean's edge, despite the uncertainty of the future? His answer is probably typical of anyone who's enjoyed the sounds, sensations and emotions of living in close proximity to the sea.

"If I had a choice, I'd never leave here."

THE GALANTI HOUSE LIES SLUMPED ON THE BEACH AS SIGHTSEERS WALK THE SHORE.

THE STORY OF CHATHAM'S NORTH BEACH　　　　　**87**

All Along The Revetment

To me, it's a personality out there, it's not just water. It has its own life, it breathes. It's going to do what it's going to do. Sometimes I hear those waves just laughing, "You poor fools! I have to do this, this is my design, and I'm going to do it. You can put up stone walls and build lighthouses, I can just eat away at them." That's what it's saying out there. I'm going to do what I'm going to do.

— Shorefront property owner Tim Pennypacker

On October 30, 1991, a violent northeaster sent 20-foot waves crashing over a weakened North Beach, destroying 16 beach camps. Thick with froth and churned a sandy brown, the angry sea attacked the vulnerable bluff at the lighthouse overlook, tearing out huge chunks of earth; asphalt from the parking lot followed. At the end of the three-day storm, the edge of the bank was 14 feet from Main Street. Seven houses were condemned, property damage was estimated at $4 million. One cottage on Andrew Harding's Lane was sheared off its foundation and sent smashing into the house up the road.

Nature was not finished with Chatham yet.

The Halloween Northeaster, the same storm that sunk a Gloucester swordfish boat as detailed in Sebastian Junger's "The Perfect Storm," was a record breaker, by far the most destructive storm since the tempest that smashed North Beach's back. Yet to some, including the Town of Chatham, it was a godsend. Although it was touch-and-go for a while, most of the North Beach camps were rebuilt, most elevated on pilings sunk 20 feet into the living beach, anchor enough to hold them

COLLAPSED SECTIONS OF THE LIGHTHOUSE OVERLOOK PARKING AFTER THE 1991 HAL-
LOWEEN NORTHEASTER.

A MASSIVE SANDBAG WALL BUILT TO PROTECT ALFRED NELSON'S HOUSE AFTER THE 1991
STORM WAS EVENTUALLY COMPLETELY BURIED BY SAND.

BREAKTHROUGH

through several subsequent storms. The coastal area was declared a federal disaster area by President George Bush, and even though erosion had been gnawing away at the lighthouse overlook bluff for weeks before the storm — the town had already drawn up plans to enhance the rip-rap that had been placed along the foot of the bank in 1931 — the federal disaster aid paid $600,000 of the $800,000 construction cost of a 600-foot long, 20-foot high revetment along what was once one of Chatham's best public beaches.

As more revetments went in after the first were built in 1988, Lighthouse Beach disappeared. By 1991 there was no beach left, and the wooden beach stairs ended in mid-air as the level of the sand dropped by a half dozen or more feet. But the wall constructed for nearly $1 million did the job and in a year, the beach was almost as wide and sandy as it was prior to the break.

Also contributing to the awesome accretion was the fact that a bridge of sand now connected South Beach to the mainland just south of the Chatham Beach and Tennis Club. Called a tombolo — a spit of sand connecting two land bodies — it opened up access to South Beach and created a huge problem with pedestrian traffic. And with the Lighthouse Beach stairs out of commission, people were trespassing on private property to get to the beach. Enter Alfred and Evelyn Nelson.

After the houses between Andrew Harding's Lane and Holway Street were lost, only the Wilsons and Rolfes carried on the battle in the courts, never with much success. The fight against the state's restrictions against revetments in some locations was inherited by the Nelsons, and their neighbors a thousand or so feet down the beach, Lewis and Bernice Hicks. Both families' homes had suffered extensive flooding during the storms of the early 1990s. Little Beach was the last eroding area without revetments because, state officials said, the area was one big sand dune.

At one point, after the stairs to Lighthouse Beach were destroyed and before the town put in a new set at the seaward end of nearby Bearse's Lane, the Nelsons opened up to pedestrians a strip of their property running between Morris Island Road and the beach. All they asked was that people stick to the path and stay off the dunes. By the end of the summer, thousands had walked to the wildly natural South Beach via the Nelsons' path.

Alfred Nelson was an elderly southern gentleman from Louisiana who had bought his house in the early 1960s. His hobby created a beach landmark: a spindly ham radio antenna mounted on an old telephone pole. He spent many evenings sitting in his radio room, facing the break, discussing his situation with friends thousands of miles away. Nelson's problem was that storms had blasted every sand dune in front of his house and the ocean was tapping on his window. After two failed attempts to get permission to build a revetment, after watching the overnight disappearance of $30,000 worth of sand, dumped on the beach in a desperate attempt to stave off erosion, Nelson finally won emergency authorization for a temporary sandbag revetment. The excavation of a huge crater oceanward of the Nelson house, into which the black body-bag like sacks were loaded, was another sober image of man's constant struggle with the sea, which Chatham at that time seemed to be losing.

But like the Lighthouse Beach revetment, the sandbags worked, although they have yet to be tested by a 100-year storm like the Halloween Northeaster.

Led by the stalwart Nick Soutter, who had become something of an all-purpose advocate for erosion victims, the Hickses and Nelsons took their petitions all the way to the U.S. Supreme Court, filing a request for review in October 1994. Soutter claimed, in his brief, that state regulations prohibiting the construction of revetments on coastal dunes had robbed his clients of the full use of their property and they were therefore entitled either to compensation for a regulatory land taking, or they should be allowed to build revetments.

Soutter also repeated his oft-asserted premise that the science backing up the state regulations was either faulty or fictitious. "There is no legitimate state purpose in [the state's] regulations," the brief claimed. "[The state] seek[s] to return the coast to a state of nature on the premise that this will protect wetlands."

A few years later, Soutter told me that when he finally got a look at the state's file that supposedly outlined the science behind the regulations, it contained a single article by coastal geologist Orin Pilkey.

"It's like two armies of ignorance grappling in the dark," he said of the regulatory process. "It's like a glass wall. Both sides can see but not hear each other."

Like most of the petitions filed every year, the Chatham erosion lawsuit was rejected by the Supreme Court. Undaunted, Soutter turned to an administrative process for appealing denials by wetland agencies, which he had previously dismissed as a waste of time and which

THE AFTERMATH OF THE 1991 STORM JUST NORTH OF THE FISH PIER.

THE STORY OF CHATHAM'S NORTH BEACH

several courts had cited as the route that must be exhausted before serious legal action could ensue. Soutter's trepidation, it turned out, was validated when the appeal was turned down. Another lawsuit was filed, but this time the property owners and state officials agreed to try mediation to settle their differences.

* * *

The Halloween Northeaster not only destroyed property; it also devastated much of Chatham's commercial fishing fleet, tossing 45-foot boats onto the shore along Aunt Lydia's Cove and sweeping away hundreds of thousands of dollars worth of lobster traps and fishing gear.

While fishermen were to face a much more severe and long-lasting crisis later in the decade when restrictions were instituted to save dwindling groundfish stocks, shoaling in the harbor continued to plague them. There were times when even shallow draft boats couldn't get to the fish pier dock to unload their catches. Fishermen resorted to offloading onto dinghies, the danger of which was illustrated when veteran fisherman Jack Our fell out of his skiff and nearly drowned in the icy water. After more than six years of study, the Army Corps of Engineers was finally prevailed upon to accept regular maintenance dredging of Aunt Lydia's Cove in 1993, but only after Congressman Studds attached a rider on a trade bill with the Baltic republic of Estonia. That, of course, led to a few snickers along the waterfront, but was touchingly remembered when the Estonian flag was hoisted at the fish pier during a celebration marking the start of $1 million dredging project on January 14, 1995.

The deep-water channel leading from the fish pier to the inlet and the Atlantic beyond shifted radically month by month, week by week. Meandering through the harbor like a huge snake, the channel strayed dangerously close to several revetments, threatening to undermine them. Over the course of a few weeks, the channel slithered away from the shores of Claflin Landing, destroyed in the Halloween Northeaster and left broken up and useless by the town, and curled toward North Beach across the harbor. It was particularly ferocious where the channel brushed up against South Beach. Much of the sand swept into the channel as the nub of the barrier spit was whittled away ended up on the new, luxurious Lighthouse Beach. Town waterways officials nearly went mad trying to keep channels marked.

It was still pretty treacherous navigating through the inlet, yet there were only a few incidents involving boats being lost or sustaining major damage while traversing the cut. In September 1988, the sportfishing boat *Michael Kevin* capsized in the surf. Fishermen on board the nearby *Hungry Eyes* rescued the crew, who miraculously escaped uninjured. Still, the incident caused a shakeup at the Chatham Coast Guard Station, which came under heavy criticism because the *Michael Kevin*'s distress call could not be answered. Low tide prevented any of the station's vessels from reaching the breach area. The result was a new station chief and a funky bright orange rigid hull inflatable (RHI) boat with a Volvo jet engine and an extremely shallow draft. Chatham eventually wound up inheriting the RHI that had been used to patrol off Kennebunkport, Maine, when George Bush was president.

* * *

When the wrecking crews began tearing down Ruth and Elwyn Perry's Andrew Harding's Lane house on September 18, 1989, there were no crowds of curious onlookers, no late summer tourists anxious for a peek at the tragedy wrought by the North Beach break. A few reporters and photographers came and went as heavy machinery made matchsticks of the 182-year-old house, one of Chatham's oldest, ordered removed as erosion continued its landward march. The contrast with the circus-like atmosphere that surrounded the collapse of the Galanti cottage was remarkable.

By 1995, nine houses were lost, and one, owned by the Whitings off Holway Street — a roadway held in place by a small, makeshift revetment built by the town's highway department — was in limbo. Over and over, the family's engineer assured town officials the approved wall would be built. South of Holway Street, a big strand of beach stretched unbroken up to the first revetment. In between looked like a surrealistic sculpture, with huge boulders standing in the water a dozen feet from the shore, looking very out of place. There were pipes that led nowhere, meadow bank and brick, an occasional remnant of the houses that once stood where the waves made their slow run up the shallow beach. It was calm there, most of the time. Even in big storms, the beach grew so wide and so protected that it eroded little. Most of the floodwaters spilled over into the low area between Andrew Harding's Lane and Holway Street during the big storms of the early '90s causing some severe flooding to a number of homes well away from the dangerous shore.

In the Halloween Northeaster, a cottage owned by James and Diana

Fitchett — who later hit the Massachusetts State Lottery for millions — was lifted off its foundation and swept into its neighbor like a plastic toy. The Fitchett house was demolished, but the Ganaway cottage, though sheared off its foundation by several inches, was not a total loss. In a job that took more than a year, the cottage was rebuilt and elevated on huge, thick wooden pilings. It was now the last house on Andrew Harding's Lane, lifted high above the ground like the crow's nest of a ship.

In 1994, the town offered homeowners who live along the shore matching grants to pay for work to floodproof buildings. The money came from the federal government's Federal Emergency Management Agency, which stepped in after the Halloween Northeaster and funneled hundreds of thousands of dollars to municipalities, homeowners and fishermen.

The town became much more active in the shoreline problem after a Coastal Erosion Advisory Committee was belatedly appointed by the selectmen in 1990. After spending a year trying to figure out its purpose, the committee was reshuffled into a much more pro-active body as a result of the first of several huge storms yet to come. Margaret Swanson, the town's director of planning and development, took over and immediately began developing a strategy to take care of the most pressing need. In 1988, the state told the BREACH group that each member would have to file an environmental impact report (EIR) to get a final revetment permit; the walls were originally built with emergency permits, and final permits were necessary, or else deed and land title problems could develop. Also, as something of an excuse for the town to spearhead the project on behalf of the property owners, the state required that the town also do an EIR for the Lighthouse Beach revetment.

In 1992, Aubrey Consulting, Inc., of Falmouth was hired to do what was to have been a management plan for the entire strip of beachfront from Minister's Point to Morris Island. It was broken into two parts: phase one was a study of the impact of the 29 revetments built from the Chatham Beach and Tennis Club north; phase two encompassed Little Beach, the Morris Island Dike and Morris Island.

The participation of Dr. David Aubrey, a world-famous scientist affiliated with the Woods Hole Oceanographic Institute, was heavy at first, but the nuts-and-bolts work — the research and development of recommendations — was done by Dr. Lee Weishar and other staff members. They came up with some interesting predictions about Chatham's shoreline which raised a few eyebrows.

While allowing that the Nauset Beach barrier beach system is cyclical in nature, they suggested that the cycle initiated in 1987 would not follow the same pattern as the one begun by the 1846 break. That's because the breaks were in different locations, two miles apart. Last century, there was more South Beach to break up and move shoreward; because of the natural littoral drift, that was good news for the Little Beach area. Since the break was farther down the beach this time, it will probably be Morris Island and Monomoy that receive the bulk of the sand once South Beach is worn down by wind and waves and migrates to the west. This creates the distinct possibility that Monomoy and South Beach may be joined, which sets up an interesting jurisdictional quandary, since the Cape Cod National Seashore, part of the U.S. Park Service, has authority over South Beach, while the U.S. Fish and Wildlife Service controls Monomoy. Eventually, though, South Beach will disappear entirely, leaving Little Beach exposed, lending urgency to the plea of homeowners for permission to build revetments.

But the report was dry and scientific, and didn't capture the reality felt by many shorefront property owners.

"To me, it's a personality out there, it's not just water," said Tim Pennpacker, a former selectman whose family owned a home adjacent to the lighthouse overlook for most of the 20th century. "It has its own life, it breathes. It's going to do what it's going to do. Sometimes I hear those waves just laughing, 'You poor fools! I have to do this, this is my design, and I'm going to do it. You can put up stone walls and build lighthouses, I can just eat away at them.' That's what it's saying out there. I'm going to do what I'm going to do."

* * *

Chatham has indeed become famous for its erosion. The Nauset Beach barrier beach system is generally referred to as the most dynamic coastal system on the east coast of the United State. It has certainly been studied by a plethora of scientists, government officials, graduate students and school children. It's been written about in dozens of magazine articles and even in poetry. The Weather Channel did a special segment on erosion in Chatham. Dr. Orin Pilkey of Duke University and Dr. Stephen Leatherman of the University of Maryland, two of the world's leading coastal geologists, have visited here and spoken to rapt audiences.

The collective experience engendered by the breakthrough has changed Chatham. Not only has the landform been altered and the sandy harbor bottom stirred up, people's attitudes have also shifted. And like the shuffling shoals that bedevil fishermen, there is no telling where loyalties will lie, who will ally with whom when the weather clears and the sun rises over the outer beach. On March 30, 1995, an unlikely alliance of Chatham town officials, Little Beach property owners, a state DEP attorney and Nick Soutter all stood together before the Cape Cod Commission in unified support of the plan to protect Little Beach. Everyone finally agreed on one thing: the enemy was the ocean, not each other.

BREAKTHROUGH

RETURN OF THE REVETMENT WARS

We're not the kind of people to be moved by anything, nature or otherwise.
— ALFRED NELSON

The cohesiveness didn't last. During the next few years, the fragile coalition of Little Beach property owners formed to secure permission to building revetments when the need came collapsed. Another Chatham erosion case was appealed to the U.S. Supreme Court, and two property owners raised resentment among residents by opposing a town and U.S. Army Corps of Engineers plan to dredge Chatham Harbor.

Months of negotiations, dozens of court motions, counter-motions and remands and hundreds of hours of discussion went into the Little Beach compromise that was finally approved in 1995 by the Cape Cod Commission, Barnstable County's land regulatory agency. The commission entered the picture to review the coastal management plan written by the town which addressed, retroactively, many of the issues raised during the revetment wars of the late 1980s. Nearly 40 seawalls were built after the breakthrough, most of them north of Little Beach, starting with the Chatham Beach and Tennis Club and ending just south of Claflin Landing. The management plan served as an environmental impact report for those revetments, and it also included the town's proposal to address the likelihood that Little Beach and areas to the south would at some point come under attack by erosion. But the proposal wasn't to the liking of the two Little Beach property owners who had suffered the most at the hands of the Atlantic, the Nelson and Hicks families.

With South Beach attached to the mainland right in front of the Nelson home, there was more sand along Little Beach than ever before. Ever cognizant of how tenuous the beach was, both families believed the only way to ensure protection of their property was to build revetments. They felt it was unfair that the town and state had allowed the beach club to build a wall — in apparent contradiction to state regulations which only permit seawalls to protect homes, not ancillary structures like tennis courts — but to repeatedly deny their requests. But officials continued to stick to the assertion that the area was a coastal dune and hard structures like revetments weren't allowed. They'd already bent the rules a bit to let the Nelsons build a huge sand bag wall, which was now buried under several feet of sand. That would have to suffice if the ocean once again knocked on their door.

There was more bending to come. After court-ordered mediation and intervention by the Cape Cod Commission, a plan was hammered out that the property owners grudgingly accepted. Calling for a revetment about half the size of those to the north, the plan set up three "trigger points." The wall couldn't be built until the beach eroded back to these points. Officials justified their slight alteration in policy in much the same way the Conservation Commission had concluded that the Wilsons and Rolfes could built walls at Andrew Harding's Lane: once the beach eroded back to the set location, the coastal dune no longer performed its function of serving as a rolling buffer between the beach and mainland. Accepting the argument that erosion to Little Beach was inevitable once South Beach broke apart, the state was willing to work toward waivers of wetland regulations to allow the wall in a coastal dune environment.

Although they grudgingly accepted the compromise, the Nelson and Hicks families, through their attorney, Nick Soutter, argued that they should be able to build the walls now and cover them up with sand. The plan's main flaw, besides the too-small size of the revetment, was that by the time the trigger points are hit, it will be too late, they said. By the time the revetments can be built, erosion will have surged ahead and their properties would be destroyed. Officials countered that the points were set sufficiently eastward to allow time for construction of the walls.

It wasn't only the Nelsons and Hicks who had doubts about the plan. There were four other properties between them, and at least two of the owners didn't see the need for a revetment and declined to go along with the plan. For months, William Doggett, who owned a home in the neighborhood and represented a loose group called the Little Beach Erosion Protection Association, worked to hold the coalition together. Many people who, like Doggett, owned property between Little Beach and Morris Island Road, saw it as the only way to ensure that at some point, their property would not be next on erosion's menu. Eventually, all of the owners signed on, but the issue still was not quite settled.

In late 1995, the focus once again shifted to the north. For several months, Holway Street took a beating. With revetments to the north and a barren stretch of shore south to just past the former location of Andrew Harding's Lane, where walls began again, during high tides and storms the tide was funneled toward the jutting point of land that was the terminus of Holway Street. Before the break, Nancy Nelson's house was three houses away from the water. With houses to the east and south gone, her home soon began to flood at high tide. On November 22, with Nelson's home under consistent attack and the end of the road in danger of succumbing, the board of selectmen declared an erosion emergency at Holway Street.

Chatham's new town manager, Thomas Groux, set things in motion, persuading voters at a January 18, 1996 town meeting to appropriate $225,000 to build a revetment to protect the end of the street, which served as access to several residences north of Holway Street. If the road was allowed to fall into the ocean, the town could be liable for depriving those property owners of their access, he said. But as usual, there were complications.

To build the revetment, an area between the end of the road and Nancy Nelson's home had to be filled. Technically, that land belonged to Hazel Witherbee, whose home was demolished several years earlier. An easement was required for the town to build the wall across her property. For several months, Witherbee declined to sign the easement, and even proposed building a boathouse on the reclaimed land. Finally, officials had enough and called a special town meeting for June 25, where voters approved taking the easement by eminent domain. Construction of the wall began on July 29, and was completed October 10.

The episode signaled the solidifying of what had been a slow shift in the town's erosion policy. It began with the construction of the Lighthouse Beach revetment, the town's first solid response to erosion, and was capped by the Holway Street wall. Although it was ostensibly built to protect a town road, its true purpose was to prevent what some officials were convinced was the certain loss of Nancy Nelson's house. Once that was gone, there was nothing to stop the ocean from eroding all the way up to Main Street. Whereas the town hadn't lifted a finger to help the Wilsons, Rolfes, Galantis and others, it was coming to the rescue of their neighbors down the beach.

Once the revetment was in place, Nancy Nelson sold her house and the new owner tore down the structure, a former boarding house enshrined in local lore as the "Indian Rubber House" because of its rambling construction. A new, modern and rather ordinary house now stands protected behind the publicly-financed seawall.

Meanwhile, even though their properties were under water, the Wilsons and Rolfes weren't finished. After exhausting their appeal options in Massachusetts, in January they asked the U.S. Supreme Court to review their case. In his motion, Soutter relied on some old arguments and dredged up a few new ones. He claimed the state ban that prevent his clients from building revetments was unscientific, that there was no basis for the dune and bank distinction, and that the town and state delayed their reviews and thus contributed to the destruction of his clients' homes. He also played a new card, claiming that the town and state had discriminated against his clients, who were non-resident property owners. Almost all of the revetments built belong to residents, he said, while almost all the revetments that were denied were for non-resident homeowners. Town officials disputed this assertion, claiming they were following objective regulations and had no control over whether a resident or non-resident owned property on a dune or bank.

With no comment, the Supreme Court declined to hear the case.

Soutter had yet to fade from the picture, as did the Nelson and Hicks families of Little Beach. In 1998, the attorney filed, on behalf of the two Little Beach owners, an objection to the town's application for a permit allowing dredging in a number of areas in Chatham Harbor. He claimed that by dredging the harbor, the town was making it more likely that Little Beach would erode. Nobody took the argument seriously — especially since the area that was going to be dredged was a mile or so from Little Beach — but the appeal threw a bureaucratic wrench into the permit process, delaying dredging for more than a year. The town eventually got the permit after an administrative law judge

STORM TIDES PICKED UP A HOUSE AT THE END OF ANDREW HARDING'S LANE AND SLAMMED IT INTO THE BUILDING BEHIND IT DURING THE 1991 HALLOWEEN STORM.

BY 1995, ONLY A REVETMENT PROTECTED THE END OF HOLWAY STREET FROM BECOMING PART OF CHATHAM HARBOR. EVENTUALLY, THE TOWN REPLACED THE REVETMENT SHOWN ABOVE WITH A LARGER WALL THAT EXTENDED MORE TO THE SOUTH, AROUND THE NELSON HOUSE (THE LAST HOME ON THE LEFT SIDE OF THE ROAD).

THE STORY OF CHATHAM'S NORTH BEACH   103

ruled the two property owners did not have standing to file an appeal. The Army Corps of Engineers began, in 2000, a regular series of projects dredging the channel that led into the fish pier.

The Nelsons vowed to stay and fight. "We're not the kind of people to be moved by anything, nature or otherwise," Alfred Nelson said.

* * * *

It's been a decade since a major coastal storm has hit Chatham. The eastern shore appears relatively stable, subject only to the seasonal comings and goings of a small amount of sand along the few areas not protected by revetments. Some of the sand from the recent dredging helped build up the beach between Andrew Harding's Lane and Holway Street, helping increase its summer popularity as a neighborhood beach. Lighthouse Beach remains wide and spacious, perhaps the town's most beautiful beach. South Beach maintains its connection to the mainland, although it has shown signs of thinning in places. It's become extremely popular with walkers and hikers, and its sandbar-rich southern tip is home to thousands of seals. In October 2001, there was more sand between the Little Beach "trigger points" — dubbed "Doggetts" after William Doggett, who assiduously takes measurements every few months — and the water than ever before.

Many of the owners who fought to build revetments have sold their homes. Chatham is a different place today than it was in 1987; there's been a shift toward more preservation, with strong organizations, such as the Friends of Chatham Waterways and the Old Village Association, emerging to fight development and retain "community character." With their opposition to construction of mini-mansions and redevelopment of homes in the Old Village, the groups would likely have had something to say about the armoring of the town's east coast, had they been around during the great revetment wars. It's clear, however, that the revetments have done their job, although whether there will be a cost — every action, after all, has an equal and opposite reaction — only the future will show.

The faces behind the drama of nature and man have changed. Nick Soutter retired to Colorado and Graham Giese retired to Truro. The Nelson and Hicks families continue to enjoy their homes. John Whelan was among those who sold their homes, as was Tim Pennypacker. Chief Barry Eldredge, Peter Ford, Alice Hiscock and Joan Wilson passed away. After making a stir with a homemade houseboat, Peter Mason sailed to Florida and faded away. Some of the players — Andrew

Young, Doug Wells, William Riley — continue to play an active role in town affairs.

As for North Beach, underlying fears of another breakthrough continue to cause anxieties for some, although the likelihood of that happening is remote (South Beach, experts agree, is where most of the action is likely to be). Nine homes succumbed to the first break, which provided the relief the harbor and ocean waters needed to maintain a natural flow. Yet the beach continues to claim victims. In November 2001, a 34-year-old man whose family owned a camp on the beach drowned after becoming disoriented after a late-night drive to the beach's tip. Almost daily the end of the beach moves, mingling with the shoals and rushing currents in a continual reshaping, a visible warning that complacency has consequences.

THE BREAK IN 1998.

Glossary

Here are definitions of some terms used throughout the book which became common parlance during erosion and revetment discussions in Chatham.

Barrier beach: A landform composed of sand dunes separated from the mainland by a body of water. A barrier beach connected to the mainland at one end is a barrier spit; a barrier beach that is not connected to the mainland is a barrier island.

Coastal bank: Under Massachusetts wetland regulations, a coastal bank is composed of till (gravel, sand, clay, etc.) left by the retreat of glaciers. It is what is generally considered upland.

Coastal dune: Dunes are composed of glacial outwash, or sand, and move in response to wind and wave action, according to Massachusetts wetland regulations.

Dredge: The deepening of a waterway using machinery, which is also referred to as a dredge. Dredging can be done by mechanical (physical digging) means or with hydraulic equipment, which removes sand via suction.

Erosion: The wearing away of a beach or upland by water, wind, or glacial ice. The process can be slow, taking place over centuries, or very fast, happening in an instant, as during a major storm.

Greenhouse effect: The slow increase in the Earth's temperature caused by the trapping of a variety of gases, mostly generated by man's industrial activities, within the atmosphere.

Hard solution: The use of permanent shoreline protection such as rock or concrete.

Littoral drift: The process by which sand is transported by off-shore currents from one shoreline to another.

Longard tube: A filter cloth, which allows water but not sand to pass through, filled with sand and placed along a beach to prevent erosion.

Revetment: A rough-face seawall built with large boulders carefully placed against upland to protect an eroding shoreline. The rough face of the structure breaks up wave action and prevents scouring at the base.

Scarp: A low steep slope along a beach created by erosion.

Seawall: Used interchangeably with revetment, although it sometimes applies to a smooth-faced wall rather than a rough-faced revetment.

Soft solution: In coastal protection, this refers to a method that is not permanent and works in harmony with the environment, such as sand-bags, which can be slit and their contents spilled out onto a beach with no adverse impact to a natural beach environment.

Syzygy: The alignment of three celestial bodies. When the sun, earth and moon are involved, the effect can cause extreme high tides.

THE BREAK IN 1990.

BREAKTHROUGH

CREDITS

Kelsey-Kennard Photographers: cover photograph, photos on pages 4, 7, 11, 22, 47 (bottom), 58, 61, 84, 87, 98, 103 (top), 105, and 108.

Illustration on page 18-19 from Barrier Beach Report by Dr. Graham Giese

Chuck Stanko: illustration on page 29.

Timothy J. Wood: photographs on pages 47 (top), 53, 66, 77, 81, 90, 93, 102 (top).

Geoff Nelson: photograph on page 88.

Copyright on all photographs and illustrations owned by creators; used with permission.

For Chatham breakthrough photos and Cape Cod airviews, contact:
Kelsey-Kennard Photographers
Box 736
Chatham, MA 02633
508-945-1931
www.capecodphotos.com

ABOUT THE AUTHOR

A native of Connecticut, Timothy J. Wood moved to Cape Cod after graduating from the University of Connecticut, where he was an editor at the daily newspaper serving the Storrs campus. He went to work for the Cape Cod Chronicle in Chatham, first in the production department, and gradually shifting over to reporting and editorial writing. Aside from a break of a few years, he's been there ever since, currently serving as the weekly newspaper's editor and Chatham reporter. "Breakthrough" was first published in 1988, and has gone through five printings, selling nearly 5,000 copies. This newest edition has been substantially revised, updated and expanded, with many new photographs, bringing the story of Chatham's battle with nature into the new millennium. Along with chronicling the town's weekly news and activity, Wood is co-founder of The Art of Charity, a foundation that has contributed more than $200,000 to local children's charities. He lives in Chatham with his wife, Jenny, and their two cats, Athena and Possum.